e-roadmapping

e-roadmapping

digital strategising
for the new economy

by

Stefan P. Bornheim

with

Jutta Weppler
and
Oliver Ohlen

with case studies from

DaimlerChrysler, getmobile.de,
GoIndustry.com and Siemens

palgrave

First published 2001 by
PALGRAVE
Houndmills, Basingstoke, Hampshire RG21 6XS and
175 Fifth Avenue, New York, N.Y. 10010
Companies and representatives throughout the world

PALGRAVE is the new global academic imprint of
St. Martin's Press LLC Scholarly and Reference Division and
Palgrave Publishers Ltd (formerly Macmillan Press Ltd).

ISBN 0–333–78695–5 hardcover

This book is printed on paper suitable for recycling and
made from fully managed and sustained forest sources.

A catalogue record for this book is available
from the British Library.

JK

Library of Congress Cataloging-in-Publication Data

Bornheim, Stefan P.
  E-roadmapping : digital strategising for the new economy /
Stefan P. Bornheim ; with assistance from Jutta Weppler and
Oliver Ohlen.
    p. cm.
  Includes bibliographical references and index.
  ISBN 0–333–78695–5
    1. Electronic commerce. 2. Business enterprises—Data
processing. I. Weppler, Jutta. II. Ohlen, Oliver. III. Title.
  HF5548.32 .B665 2001
  658.8'4—dc21   2001021887

Editing and origination by
Aardvark Editorial, Mendham, Suffolk

10 9 8 7 6 5 4 3 2 1
10 09 08 07 06 05 04 03 02 01

Printed and bound in Great Britain by
Creative Print & Design (Wales), Ebbw Vale

CONTENTS

Contents

List of Figures

List of Figures

LIST OF TABLES

Navigation through the book

The set-up of this book is rather modular. Each of the five chapters can be read by itself and, of course, they can be read in any order. Nevertheless, for the reader planning to read the whole book the recommendation is to do so in a sequential manner, as the early part of the book is broad based before coming to detailed e-strategy questions. The benefit from reading in sequence is expected to be greater than that derived from chapter-jumping.

Readers interested in partial aspects of the book may use the following elaboration to detect where to go for their interest:

- Chapters 1 and 2 to find out about the *general Digital Economy* trends and the changes in competition and *competitive behaviour*.

- Chapter 3 for those interested in understanding and applying our *e-roadmapping strategising tool*.

- Chapter 4 for a variety of *e-business case studies*. These case studies range from business-to-consumer (B2C) to business-to-business (B2B) and cover start-up as well as corporate e-business projects.

- Chapter 5 for a glimpse of the *promises of the future*; readers interested in the future of business and technology applications should direct their attention to this chapter.

The underlying academic research of e-roadmapping

This book is a practitioner-oriented book and therefore will not dwell on research methodologies, sample sizes, and so on. Yet, our readers are entitled to know what the academic grounding of this publication is.

This book rests on over 18 months of academic research at the University of St. Gallen and subsequent consulting and executive teaching in the field.

In the initial phase of the tool development many interviews were held with traditional corporations as well as with start-up companies. These interviews gave a clearer understanding of the challenges at hand and provided many insights into the real problems of companies dealing with the emerging Digital Economy.

Once the basic concepts were developed and put in place, another round of interviews was conducted to 'beef up' these concept categories and to test these constructs.

After completing the tool-set a final empirical test was done through a quantitative survey of European B2B marketplaces through which the tool was tested and validated in detail.

Further reality checks were then achieved through applying the e-roadmapping tool in a number of strategy workshops with various companies, as well as using the concepts in an executive teaching environment.

Thanks to...

As always a book of this nature and magnitude could not have happened without a substantial team effort. I am particularly thankful to my co-authors Jutta and Oliver, who endured my very special writing mode and whose endless constructive input and willingness to discuss parts of the concept were crucial to the completion of the book. Without their help in further developing and refining the concepts, many questions would still be unanswered.

Many thanks also to my publishing editor, Stephen Rutt, and his team at Palgrave, who from the proposal stage onwards displayed absolute professionalism in their conduct and were very constructive in helping to publish this book on time.

I also owe a debt of gratitude to Winfried Ruigrok at the International Management Institute at the University of St. Gallen, as well as the GFF research fund of the university for their support during this period.

A great many thanks also to the companies contributing e-business case studies. Both the getmobile.de team and Paul Vega with GoIndustry were superb in their turnaround time and ability to produce fascinating case studies. At Siemens my thanks go to Stefan Holler and his team, who produced a case of great depth and tremendous complexity. I also thank Olaf Koch and Mitchell Mackey at DaimlerChrysler's DCX-Net in Stuttgart for setting up this co-operative effort and Keith Helfrich and his team at the Five Star Market Center in Auburn Hills for so promptly delivering the actual case. Lastly, I am grateful to Johannes Schmohl from marchFIRST who without hesitation was willing to share a great many insights on how to implement successful e-business projects.

A last and very special thanks goes to my fiancée for unconditional support, incredible patience and continuous inspiration during the long and occasionally tedious period of writing this book.

S.B.

LIST OF ABBREVIATIONS

AIP	ASP infrastructure provider
ASP	application service provider/provision
B2B	business-to-business
B2C	business-to-customer/business-to-consumer
BIF	business integration framework
C2C	customer-to-customer/consumer-to-consumer
CAGR	compounded annual growth rate
CRM	customer relationship management
CSF	critical success factor
DSP	dealership systems provider
EAI	enterprise application integration
EDI	electronic data interchange
eRI	e-roadmapping index
ERP	enterprise resource planning
EV	enterprise value
FSMC	Five Star Market Center
GSM	global system mobile
HTML	hypertext markup language
I&C	information and communication
IP	Internet protocol
IPO	Initial Public Offering
ISP	Internet service provider
ISV	independent software vendor
IT	information technology
LTM	last twelve months

MRO	maintenance, repair and operations
MRP	material requirement planning
MSDW	Morgan Stanley Dean Witter
OEM	original equipment manufacturer
PDA	personal digital assistant
PO	purchase order
RFQ	request for quotation
SBS	Siemens Business Services
SCM	supply chain management
SD	systems dynamics
SME	small and medium-sized enterprises
SMS	short message service
T-tax	transaction tax
UCS	User Centre Services
UMTS	universal mobile telecommunications system
USP	unique selling point
WAP	wireless application protocol
XML	extensible markup language

Much has been written in recent years about the rise of the Internet, the World Wide Web, and the changes it will bring about to all of our lives and the manifestation of these changes through the New or Digital Economy. The issue is at the forefront of government policy debates (Gore, Digital Economy II): on one hand, the Internet revolution is seen as a source of fundamental technological, economic and social changes that foster innovation, productivity gains and new employment opportunities; on the other hand, the accelerated globalisation of business and the worldwide access to information, product and service offerings raise direct challenges to governments in terms of tax collection and tax competition between nations (Bishop, 2000). At the turn of the millennium, there has been a rapid, often unanticipated rise of new winners across a wide range of industries. Many incumbent one time leaders have had to learn that their traditional business models were obsolete, their organisations too inert, and their physical resources that once defined their competitive advantage had become a liability. At the same time, consultant firms do not tire of finding fancier phrases every day for packaging their advice on how to cope with these changes. And academics are baffled by this new phenomenon. All are stakeholders in the business community, realising the need for maintaining an intelligible opinion on coping with change even though a satisfactory roadmap for understanding the phenomenon remains blatantly absent.

Considering the lack of concrete tools for executives and entrepreneurs in their current struggle to strategise in the new, digitised economy, this book introduces a new tool-set for capturing this perplexing phenomenon. It will allow company leaders to grasp the landscape and subsequently plot their route through this new territory.

This book helps to explain the fundamental changes the Digital Economy brings about and outlines the consequences for corporations. Specifically, assumptions about competition will be questioned and rendered outdated, while new modes of competitive thinking will be introduced. In addition to competitive thinking, modes of performance measurement will be examined and complemented with a new breed of value metrics.

The book is structured as follows: In Chapter 1, the challenges of change, that is the foundations of the Digital Economy, will be displayed: subsequent to defining the Digital Economy, fundamental patterns and profit models that determine the shape of this new phenomenon will be detailed. Thereafter, the following basic elements will be introduced as the foundations of our framework for navigating through the Digital Economy: new value metrics, technology, customer centricity and organisational configuration. These elements are abstracted dimensions which through our research we found helpful in explaining the phenomenon in a number of industries such as financial services and telecommunications. Whether these are the right or the only dimensions for explaining the Digital Economy remains to be seen – time will tell.

In Chapter 2, the process dimension in the context of competition is introduced. In particular, the blurring of, for example, industry boundaries and the emergence of new communities of co-opetition will be examined. The need for speed of innovation, conception and execution is placed in a strategic context, and lastly, the major shift from resource-based to information-based competition is sketched. This chapter leaves the meta-level of assumptions and aims to elucidate the major context changes, particularly as they pertain to the changing rules of the game. We pose questions that illuminate the change brought about with new performance measurements, which signify a substantive change in the nature of competition.

Chapter 3 introduces e-roadmapping, an intellectual tool for understanding the issue of digital strategising. e-roadmapping as a process-oriented tool begins with a mapping of the digital landscape to help determine of which 'new game' a firm is becoming a part or is deliberately deciding to join. Once the arena of competition is determined the new business models are delineated. The final step of e-roadmapping helps to define the steps on a firm's way to transformation, that is of becoming an eConomy-savvy organisation. (See Figure 0.1 for a visualisation of Chapters 1–3)

Chapter 4 is divided into sub-chapters which overlay the e-roadmapping process in the concrete context of e-business examples from two large corporations, DaimlerChrysler and Siemens, and two start-ups, getmobile.de and GoIndustry. A concrete e-business implementation guide is provided up-front by marchFIRST.

Insights gained from these showcases are directly transferable to the reader's practice. These exemplars are excerpted from the current portfolio of e-activities of the firms. The contributions from these companies come from very divergent lines of business as they represent Old Economy vs. New Economy, and physical production vs. service solution companies.

We therefore offer a broad range of examples in which the e-roadmapping tool can be utilised.

In the closing chapter, the lessons learnt from the application of the tool in these various contexts are then synthesised in the 'Visions for the Future' part which describes our thinking on some emerging mega-trends.

References

Bishop, M. (2000) The mystery of the vanishing tax payer. *The Economist*, **8155** (29 January): 3–9.

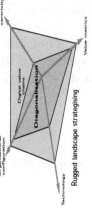
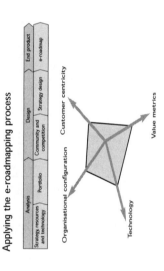

Figure 0.1 Roadmap of Chapters 1–3

Challenges of Change

CHAPTER CONTENTS

In this chapter we will review some of the more basic contributions to the New Economy debate, including a definitional overview, an evaluation of some emerging digital patterns and a summary of changes between the traditional and the Digital Economy. This analysis leads on to an outline of the challenges ahead which are tackled in the ensuing chapter.

Literature review

There is a broad consensus that the emergent Digital Economy will cause profound social, technological, and economic changes (Orlikowski and Iacono, 2000). The fast-changing, intensely inter-linked environment of the digital age creates multiple challenges for corporations: rapid technological obsolescence, increased complexity, rapidly changing industry settings and value drivers, disintermediation potential, accelerated time-to-market cycles, the emergence of new market spaces, the shift from resource-based to information-based competition, and so on (Marshall et al., 1999).

Much of the contemporary, buzzword-rich discourse about the Digital Economy is often misleading because it creates the impression that we are facing an exogenous, inevitable, and unstoppable phenomenon. On the contrary, the Digital Economy is not just happening out there. It is rather an ongoing and complex product, which is invented, constructed, and constantly modified by human beings (Orlikowski and Iacono, 2000). From an economic point of view, the Digital Economy is shaped by new start-up

companies as well as established corporations as they develop and implement sophisticated information technology, new business models, and innovative organisational and inter-organisational practices (Aldrich, 1999).

Before taking a closer look at this new, fast-changing phenomenon and
its profound implications for nearly all kinds of businesses, one has to
define what the Digital Economy is, what its sub-sectors are and what the
technological enablers are.

Definitions

In publications, the terms New Economy and Information Economy are
often used interchangeably with Digital Economy. These are overlapping
but signify different concepts. The New Economy focuses on macroeco-
nomic effects of business activities that are enabled by information technology (IT) – emphasising high growth, low inflation, and low
unemployment (Kling and Lamb, 2000, p. 296). In contrast, the concept
Information Economy deals with the development, production, and sale of
information goods, for example books, databases, magazines, software,
stock quotes, and so on. For example, publishing companies or providers
of content on the Internet are a part of this concept. In short, information
is anything that can be digitised – encoded as a stream of bits (Shapiro and
Varian, 1999).

Kling and Lamb (2000) provide a holistic approach and define the
Digital Economy as follows:

> the Digital Economy includes goods or services whose development,
> production, sale, or provision is critically dependent upon digital tech-
> nologies. (p. 297)

The authors acknowledge that the Internet is the major enabler of growth
in electronic business. Nonetheless, proprietary networks such as
corporate intranets, electronic data interchange (EDI), and so on, which
will continue to play an important role in the next years, are also part of
this concept. We find this to be an adequate working definition of the
Digital Economy for the purposes of this book. Naturally, one could take
this further and posit that such confinement is unnecessary as no
company will be able to exist in the near future that has not embraced the
Digital Economy.

The Digital Economy according to Kling and Lamb then is based on
four sub-sectors (Kling and Lamb, 2000, pp. 297–8):

▪ *Highly digital goods and services* are those goods that are delivered digitally and services where a substantial portion is delivered digitally (for example online information services, electronic journals, software sales, and so on).

▪ *Mixed digital goods and services* include the retail sale of tangible goods, such as books or flowers over the Internet, as well as services such as travel reservations.

▪ *IT-intensive services or goods production* include services that depend critically on IT to be provided (for example complex engineering design) and tangible goods where IT is critical in their production (for example computerised control of chemical plants).

▪ *The parts of the IT industry that support one of the above-mentioned three segments.*

Digital patterns and laws

After the definition of the Digital Economy phenomenon it is now important to concretise this understanding. The core focus of this analysis centres around the abstraction of the patterns of economic activity and profit models. In the short duration of the Digital Economy revolution the following five law-like patterns have been applied in attempts to explain economic activity in the Digital Economy (cf. Kelly, 1998; Aldrich, 1999; Shapiro and Varian, 1999).

Coase's Law

The economist Coase's primary postulate is that transactions are conducted where the *cost of the transaction* is the lowest: the transaction can in principle be conducted through hierarchies, that is organisations, or in markets (Coase, 1937). As the cost of transactions decreases through the progress of information and communication technologies the push towards market clearing mechanisms increases. For example, the transaction costs of purchasing products and services are being reduced by up to 60 per cent through the use of e-procurement technologies (Woodall, 2000). As a consequence, the average size of organisations tends to decrease as more transactions can be cleared through the market, that is, outsourced to specialised partners.

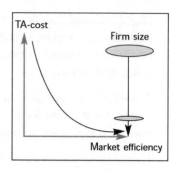

Coase
Corporations exist because the internal
transaction and coordination costs are lower
than in open market

Gilder's Law

The technologist Gilder suggests that *communication capacity* will triple every 12 months at constant cost. Bandwidth will not be the bottleneck but the standard leading to a convergence of cell phones and organisers as well as to the integration of multimedia offerings in mobile devices. For example, the UMTS (universal mobile telecommunications system) standard multiplies the communication capacity that we experience with the GSM standard as of today. By the year 2005, more people in the world are expected to access the Internet via mobile devices than via the PC (Kehoe, 2000).

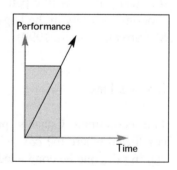

Gilder
Communications capacity will triple
every 12 months at constant cost

Metcalfe's Law

Metcalfe, the inventor of the Ethernet and founder of 3Com, determined that the *value of a network* increased as the square of the number of users. Thus, additional users are attracted to connect to the network resulting in a virtuous cycle of positive feedback. This phenomenon has important implications for corporations competing in network markets. Positive feedback works to the advantage of big networks and to the detriment of smaller networks. As a consequence, the big networks keep on growing while the smaller networks enter into a vicious cycle of negative feedback (Shapiro and Varian, 1999). Classic examples of this phenomenon are the competition between the Windows operating system from Microsoft and Apple's operating system or the VHS vs. Betamax standard battle. While in the traditional economy value is derived from scarcity, in the network economy critical mass supersedes scarcity as a source of value (Zerdick et al., 1999).

Metcalfe
Value of networks increases as the
square of the number of participants

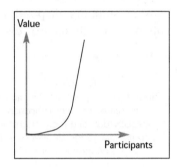

Moore's Law

One of the Intel founders – G. Moore – observed that *computer processor performance* for transport, storage and processing of information doubled roughly every 18 months at constant cost. For example, one PC from the year 1998 would have been able to control and to navigate the whole Apollo moon landing mission (Zerdick et al., 1999).

Moore
Performance for transport, storage and
processing of information doubles every
18 months at constant cost

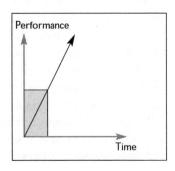

Ricardo's Law

Transposing the economist Ricardo's Law into today's competitive land-scape suggests that through utilisation of Internet technologies, *focusing on core activities* (that is one's comparative advantage) becomes much easier and desirable. All non-core activities can be acquired from partners, leading not only to efficiency boosts within the organisation but within the whole economic system. A recent example is the outsourcing contract between Deutsche Telekom and the Swiss Danzas Group, a subsidiary of Deutsche Post: beginning in September 2000, Danzas will take over the whole range of logistics services from Deutsche Telekom such as ware-housing, shipping, disposal, and so on, leading to an outsourcing contract volume of 1 billion euros over the next five years.

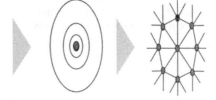

Ricardo
The outsourcing of non-core activities increases efficiency through specialisation and focus therefore increases value for all players in the economic web

After this brief overview of five patterns of applicability in the Digital Economy, it is now important to outline company-specific implications, through detailing the *profit models* of the future (cf. Figure 1.1), and contrasting them with the old (cf. Figure 1.2). This way, the change in profit models can be shown and the organisational consequences can be outlined.

In the past, it typically sufficed to contrast product- or project-specific costs and revenues, allowing easy determination of the break-even, ROI ratios, and so on. In the Digital Economy, companies often enter markets through offering standardised products, competing in these commodities not for price, but for the first contact with the customer. Subsequently, profit will be primarily generated through *marketing of additional services* such as financing, insurance, and so on; competition therefore is not differenti-ated any more on price, but on pre- or after-sales services. For example, carmakers are increasingly moving into the aftermarket in order to capture downstream revenues in service, parts, and ancillary products. Moreover, through the use of sophisticated customer relationship management (CRM) and data warehousing technologies, companies will be able to differentiate themselves from the competition in terms of customer knowledge, customer service, respect for customer privacy, and the establishment of

New profit models emerge

The second generation marketplaces need to do more than just bring down prices: they need to add value

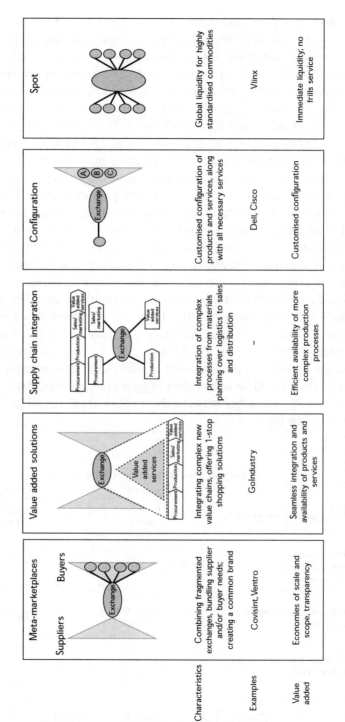

	Meta-marketplaces	Value added solutions	Supply chain integration	Configuration	Spot
Characteristics	Combining fragmented exchanges, bundling supplier and/or buyer needs; creating a common brand	Integrating complex new value chains, offering 1-stop shopping solutions	Integration of complex processes from materials planning over logistics to sales and distribution	Customised configuration of products and services, along with all necessary services	Global liquidity for highly standardised commodities
Examples	Covisint, Ventro	GoIndustry	–	Dell, Cisco	Vlinx
Value added	Economies of scale and scope, transparency	Seamless integration and availability of products and services	Efficient availability of more complex production processes	Customised configuration	Immediate liquidity; no frills service

Figure 1.1   Second generation profit models

customer trust (Siebel and House, 1999). The generated information serves as a basis to maximise the value of a retained customer by offering *life-cycle sensitive solutions*. Profit maximisation therefore is customer- not product-focused, yet this may require substantial up-front investments.

Traditionally, competitive advantage could be achieved through early following, as not necessarily the pioneers but the fast followers were mostly successful (Utterback, 1994). In the Digital Economy, the *capacity and speed of innovation* will determine a firm's position of market competitiveness. Yet, it is the ability to *quickly scale the product* that will lead to market dominance. And once such position of innovation and dominance is achieved, followers will encounter a hard path to success. Corporations that are first in a market have tremendous advantages: being the first mover allows companies to quickly gain ownership of scarce brand recognition and to attract a disproportionate share of partner attention, capital, and talent. For example, Amazon.com has been able to brand its business as the online bookstore, while powerful incumbents such as Barnes & Noble that entered the online market later have serious problems catching up.

Lastly, one should be aware that the classic inter-mediation function will become obsolete, if the inter-mediating company cannot generate substantial, additional network utility. What car dealer five years ago would have suspected a software company such as Microsoft Corp. with its subsidiary Carpoint.com would be one of their biggest competitors today?

A summary of changes between the traditional and the Digital Economy is exhibited in Figure 1.2.

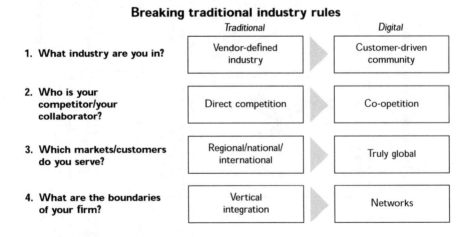

Figure 1.2   Playing the digital game

Reiterating the earlier point, just producing commodities is no longer sufficient, as additional services and customer life-cycle-encompassing products are emerging revenue drivers. Major challenges for corporations are outlined in the following:

■ How can new *customer behaviour* be segmented into meaningful clusters and how can these customer needs be addressed in an efficient way? Based on the new customer needs, what further competencies will need to be aligned and how can the customer relationship best be managed over the customer life cycle?

An Internet retailer utilising the personal shopping history to detect patterns of preference and subsequently make new purchase suggestions to the customer will, for example, give the customer the feeling of a good understanding of needs and this may ultimately lead to repeat purchases. Getmobile.de is an example of a firm that started on the basis of the (newly) perceived need of customers requiring transparency in the market of mobile communications. Based on this need the complete competencies were then aligned in a new value chain and subsequently offered to the customers. Questions and examples like these will be classified as related to the dimension we named *customer centricity and total customer experience.*

■ What are the steering and control mechanisms to conceptualise corporate success and to ensure speed in execution?

In a broad range of industries, corporations might need to modify the underlying technical, organisational, and business metrics that govern their development path in the digital environment. Questions and issues like the one above will be dealt with in a category we named *value metrics.*

■ How can *competitive leads* be maintained in the long term and constant innovation be fostered?

Brokat AG, for example, started as a secure transaction company focusing on the issue of security in the Internet. A competitive lead was achieved through superior technology, yet the understanding materialised that such capability could be used as a stepping stone to deliver secure transaction through all intra- and inter-organisational electronic channels. Questions of innovation and technology will be summarised in our *technology and innovation capabilities* category.

■ What *organisational routines* are necessary to manage the new competency alliances, the new customer relationship and the own innovation capabilities?

The last category, named *organisational configuration*, integrates organisational and management questions, like the one stated above.

The above questions then lead us to the four central dimensions of change in the digital economy:

- Customer centricity and total customer experience
- Value metrics, including online performance, valuation of business options, and scalability of business propositions
- Technology and innovation capabilities
- Organisational configuration, routines, and glue.

We propose to concentrate these four dimensions into a strategy web (Figure 1.3). This web may serve as a tool to locate corporations in the digital landscape and to determine their relative position in comparison to competitors or best practice benchmarks. In the forthcoming sections, the suggested grid will serve as the underlying rationale to comprehend and to explain some of the major developments resulting from the emerging digital economy.

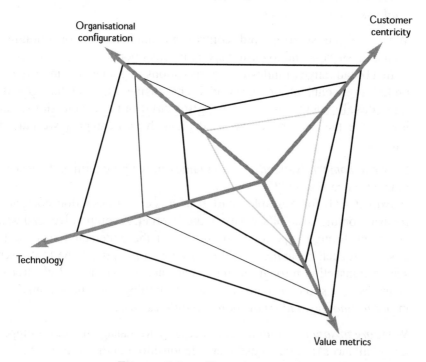

Figure 1.3   The strategy web

With an understanding of the strategic questions of tomorrow, we will now need to take a closer look at some particular elements of these future strategic issues. By breaking some of these issues into sub-issues the underlying dimensions will become more transparent.

From ERP to EAI and ASP

Enterprise resource planning systems have been becoming of ever greater economic importance since their inception, for example, in the case of SAP since the early 1980s. Some of the current major players include Computer Associates, JD Edwards, Oracle, PeopleSoft, SAP, and Software AG. Most of these players initially came out of a specific area of software like production (SAP), databases (Oracle) or human resources (People-Soft) and subsequently evolved into fully fledged enterprise resource planning programs. Due to the nature of their product intention and the industry heterogeneity, most of this software was designed in highly complex models and to this day remains incompatible in most cases. Once such a system had been implemented, proprietary connections could be established to top tier customers and suppliers.

Yet, today's business environment requires open communication interfaces and compatible languages over an open channel like the Internet. These market requirements led to the creation of EAI (enterprise application integration) companies such as NEON and others which simply created interfaces that allowed modules of one proprietary software to talk to modules of other proprietary software. That is to say, EAI software allows the utilisation of a standard exchange platform, that is the Internet, to transfer divergently formatted content.

The next logical step in this equation of open exchanges and compatible formats was to outsource some of these applications and parts of this content. With a globally open platform like the Internet it becomes no longer a necessity to host many of the required applications inhouse. Application service providers (ASPs) offer companies to buy access over the Internet to a certain application, with a specified number of users, for an agreed time frame. This allows the ASPs to realise scale economies in purchasing the original applications, whereas the user benefits from purchasing the exact quantities and times of usage for the specific application without a high up-front investment into a particular application. As of today, major players in this market are companies such as Corio, USinternetworking, Qwest, and Oracle.

If we now take our strategy web to plot the original ERP value proposition and the subsequent enhancements made through EAI and ASP, one may appreciate the possible benefits better.

On the first axis, *customer centricity*, the ERP system advanced the previous paper-based systems significantly and eased the lives of many in the enterprise by facilitating better process tracking and greater transparency. With the advent of EAI the customer focus is hardly altered; only with the availability of software and content ASPs is the ultimate customer focus available. The customer can choose content and product according to specifications as technological interfaces are standardised.

In terms of *value metrics*, the users obtained little new benefit from installing one system or the other as all systems were fairly proprietary and closed. Benefits in these regards were mainly to be realised through the producers/vendors who had zero marginal cost in scaling this software product. With EAI the scale potential also reaches the customers, but yet remained confined to existing and previously installed software. The availability of ASP generates many possibilities even for the organisations merely applying the technology: utilisation of a greater learning curve through experience sharing, and so on.

The initial *technology* proposition of course was the main enhancement of ERP software, while the ensuing revisions remained marginal in nature. Nevertheless, the benefits to users to be materialised were enormous. EAI opens venues of interfaces to technologies previously not attainable; processes can be extended rather than redesigned and content functionalities can be added at ease. ASP models enhance the technology only marginally; ASP mostly reverses the centre of technology instalments from the enterprise to the network. The question of *organisational configuration* was also rather large through ERP. Many processes had to be adapted to standards provided by the ERP vendors, yet general efficiencies could be enhanced and standardised. EAI has little impact on the organisational structures and routines. The technological glue it provides marginally extends to the organisation, only insofar as previously (technologically) separate processes can now be integrated into one process. ASPs bring about a more significant impact since not only technology but also contents can be located outside of the boundaries of the organisation. And while internal processes may remain intact, the input of external content requires new content standards and quality monitoring.

Figure 1.4 visualises the relative positions of the above displayed development stages from ERP systems to EAI and ASP in our strategy web.

In general, it may be said that EAI enhances technology and organisation through open standards and multiple possible communication plat-

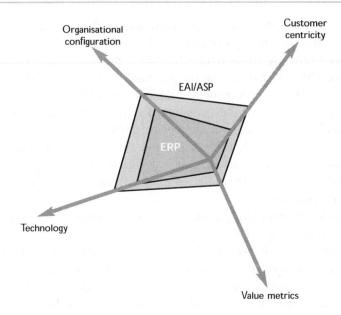

Figure 1.4   From ERP to EAI and ASP

forms, in addition to availing scale advantages to customers through the openness to other platforms/standards (value metrics). The ASP value proposition puts customer interest first, supplementing it with great technological options and superior scale advantages to user and provider. The future of what currently is known as ERP will in our opinion be open standard core process engines, which will be connected to outsourced content and technology applications. This scenario allows the organisation to model its internal processes inhouse with open engines, and connect any non-core content and technology easily via standard interfaces or platforms, and communication networks.

From e-commerce to m-commerce, WAP and UMTS

The Internet started to become of commercial interest with the advent of electronic commerce. And while no generally agreed definition exists, the general understanding entails the sale of goods and services through the Internet. For many firms, that meant and means selling traditional product and service offerings via a new sales channel. A classic example would be catalogue retailers such as Otto in Germany or Land's End in the US. Both of these firms (initially) just transferred their coloured catalogue to a new medium – the Internet – and continued selling the same content to the same audience, just through an additional sales channel.

For other firms, it meant remodelling their processes and organisations so as to be able to capitalise on the potential of the Internet through new and unique offerings. A good example is an airline like Germany's Lufthansa. They realised the potential of cost savings and sales channel enhancement by conducting a number of transactions online and to this day they continue to push as many processes as possible on to the Internet for the customer to take care of, that is, if you need a flight reservation or a weekend special offer, the online offering will easily take you through all required process steps.

And some players merely came into existence through the evolution of the Internet, offering services unheard of before. Good examples of this category are ChateauOnline or AutoScout whose mission is to provide a product depth unknown before and transparent information unseen before. In the end, it meant for all players attaining a capability to go on the Internet and offer their old, remodelled or new services through standardised formats. Many technological advances have since been made but the basic premise remains the same.

What now is becoming known as m-commerce seems like the next step of electronically distributed economic activity. Mobile commerce implies the utilisation of a mobile device somewhere in the economic activity process. It means making available information on the Internet to WAP-capable (wireless application protocol) mobile devices. The Internet part of this mobile commerce equation requires little adaptation. It is the front-end device that needs to provide more than the existing capabilities. Given the current size of data transmission over GSM lines (9600 kb/sec) it is fairly evident that most of the currently available graphics, extensive processes, and fancy for, for example, flash technologies will not be suitable for m-commerce. At the current speeds of mobile transmissions most WAP services can merely offer little bits of information, with as few graphics as possible and no colour. Complex transaction processes and routines are also not suitable for WAP-enabled m-commerce; new ways for conducting mobile transactions need to be conceived. Despite these many limitations with the current technology, most firms understand WAP-engagements as testing grounds for the coming battle with UMTS technology (Universal Mobile Telecommunications System). UMTS technology will allow far greater transmission rates for mobile phones and can therefore display most of what is currently available on the Internet through access with a traditional fixed line browser. UMTS is two to three years away in most European countries, but with the current exorbitant licence bidding and the absolute need for quick returns on these investments, we may expect to see a grand offensive on the part of the telecommunication providers to capture large chunks of this UMTS-enabled m-commerce market.

Interesting to note in this m-commerce context is the leading role that Europe as a geographical region plays. As with the GSM standard over a decade ago, European regulators and telecommunication companies (providers and producers) agreed early on the UMTS standard, while this battle for standards, for example, in the US, has not been waged to the extent of agreeing on one definite standard. This lack of agreement on standards has already put the US behind in current mobile technology, as literally very few regions carry common technological standards, leading to very little evolution on the technological side or subsequent design of applications for use with these varying standards. This can be understood particularly well in the context of the required investments for such applications and the inherent limitations to the use of such technology. Moreover, Europe displays a higher mobile phone penetration as of today: almost 70 per cent of the population in the Scandinavian countries owns a cell phone and over 50 per cent in Italy, compared with just over 30 per cent in the US (Kehoe, 2000). Thus, Europe is leading the pack on the m-commerce front, yet the full potential of UMTS applications remains to be seen. Nonetheless, mobile devices are expected to become important transaction machines or the electronic money of the future. For example, according to a study of market analyst Datamonitor, by the year 2005 over 20 million Europeans will conduct their banking via mobile devices.

In terms of our strategy web we would suggest scoring m-commerce and its subsequent applications as follows: on the first axis, *customer centricity*, m-commerce as an advancement to electronic commerce puts the customer in an even more powerful situation of deciding when and what to see and buy. Adding UMTS possibilities leaves the customer centricity intact, yet adds even more possibilities of information sourcing, value exchanging and generation. In terms of *value metrics*, the standard set by the achievements of the e-commerce wave are already fairly high. Benefits and possibilities still seem endless and will be further enhanced by UMTS. The initial *technology* proposition of course was also already fairly high; adding WAP and UMTS capabilities elevates this dimension to a premier position. That is to say, Internet technology enabled the convergence of previously mostly proprietary standards. Only with the market pull (demand) of standardised technologies was evolution of hypertext markup language (HTML), Java and now XML as unique standards for online communication possible. The question of *organisational configura-*

tion is not so easily answered. First, the Internet (r)evolution was only made possible through the emergence of a new breed of start-ups. These companies are remarkably different from existing corporations and therefore electronic commerce created completely new organisations rather than just innovation of existing ones. Nevertheless, the changes e-commerce brought about surely are changing organisational routines, through, for example, the availability of electronic workflow business rules, rather than paper-based authorisation, and so on.

Incumbents who engaged in electronic commerce activities applied various models for doing so. After a number of years of experience two observations have emerged: first the realisation that regardless of the nature of the electronic commerce project one is starting, these e-commerce activities are at all cost to be kept far away from the existing organisation. And second, keeping the e-activities away can take two forms: namely as a dot-corp, that is separate unit but within the boundaries of the existing organisation (for example Dell's dot-corp group Dell Online); or as a dot-com, which means taking the venture outside of the organisational boundaries to simulate start-up conditions as closely as possible (for example P&G's dot-com venture reflect.com). The thoughts that have been depicted in this section are summarised in Figure 1.5.

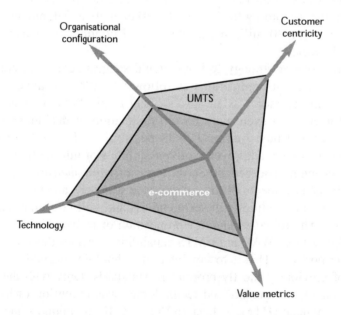

Figure 1.5   From e-commerce to m-commerce, WAP and UMTS

From mere information access to total transparency and 1-2-1 marketing

In the early days of the Internet, the days when telnet and later the gopher was used to view remote information, the main purpose of putting something on the Internet, was to inform other people. Universities utilised the medium to provide an assembly of thoughtful resources while firms displayed product or just company information. Naturally, the introduction of graphical interface browsers did not change that setting and these intentions over night. Only slowly did people realise that information provision and access was just a possible first step. Adding transaction features, a new breed of companies now known as electronic intermediaries emerged, providing customers with timely and transparent information about products and services at usually little or no cost for this particular service. With customers offering insights into some of their preferences and behaviours – in return for a free, unbiased, timely, objective, and transparent service not available anywhere else – companies now realised the possibility of serving customers even better through more accurate segmenting and through better understanding of customer needs. This allowed companies to create market push mechanisms going as far as the ability to address customers on an individual, one-to-one basis.

Our strategy web suggests the following scoring model for this category on our four axes.

On the first axis, *customer centricity* clearly is the main tenet of this category. The Internet enabled new modes of access to information, enhancing almost any sort of information needs substantially. The emergence of consumer-to-consumer intermediaries such as Epinions.com added transparency as a major feature and this again enabled customers significantly. Adding market push capabilities may not delight all customers, but it surely put the individual customer needs first. In terms of *value metrics*, we can surely suggest an objectification of information, yet that in itself does not signify a better value; however, the application possibilities of that sort of transparent information does reduce traditional inefficiencies and pricing disparities. The value add from the infomediary capabilities stage to the 1-2-1 market push stage is fairly insignificant. The initial *technology* proposition of this advancement is marginal. The application of these concepts brought about new insights and possibilities, yet the availability of this better, deeper, and more accurate information about customer behaviour and demands was only possible through the convergence of the Internet as a medium and data warehousing and data mining techniques. The value added from transparency enhancement to 1-2-1 marketing was negligible. The question of *organisational configuration is* particularly for this category an interesting one. If we look through the eyes of the consumer, the enhancements are clearly measurable yet the impact of this evolution from supply push to demand pull are not fully clear yet. The potential this demand pull could have on how consumer behaviour will become organised is tremendous. Yet, as this influences substantial parts of consumer behaviour, the steps taken are fairly linear and show the path of gradual adaptation. For example, first people start using the information source randomly to get informed on certain aspects of a purchase. The second step is the full integration of this available objectified information into the purchasing cycle. And third, people not only inform themselves through the new medium, they start conducting business and doing transactions via the Internet. This path can be observed, for example in the car buying segment in the US.

On the business-to-business side, the utility of better and transparent information has been a somewhat mixed bag as organisations usually structure their purchasing efforts and therefore use other means than just divergent information providers. Organisations have capitalised on better information by standardising their purchases and their processes, by bundling of volume, and by better parameterisation of articles. Utilisation

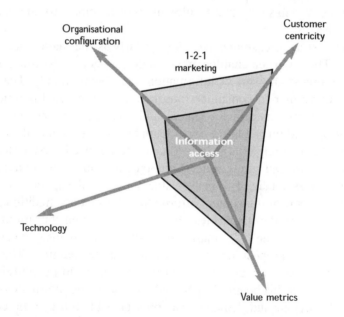

Figure 1.6　　From information access to total
transparency and 1-2-1 marketing

of better information can therefore be best observed in the context of standardised procurement software or in commodity markets such as chemdex.com (chemicals) or freemarketsonline.com (surplus sales). These marketplaces combine objectified information with transaction facilities.

To rate the overall enhancements is therefore combining reality with future potential for the business-to-consumer part, and integrating information with transaction facilities on the business-to-business side. Figure 1.6 visualises the elaborated changes in the strategy web.

From hierarchies to networks and digital value chains

Another trend manifesting over the last years is that of the diminishing influence of hierarchical organisations. And while the last waves of corporate restructuring in the early 1990s brought about a de-layering and reduction of structures, much of the old control and command philosophy remained. To this day, many organisations are organised in such a manner and for many large-sized companies in certain industries, hierarchical organisations will remain the dominant form of organisation. Yet, at the same time, certain forms of networks started arising. The early forms of networks were at the inter-organisational level. Complementary suppliers worked together to fulfil certain end-customer needs, or regionally separate firms collaborated to enhance their reach, and so on. The most recent form of networks has been the integration of, for example, purchasing capabilities of competing firms such as DaimlerChrysler, Ford, and GM in non-strategic product categories. These corporations announced the launch of a new venture that combines the assets of Ford's, GM's, and Daimler-Chrysler's purchasing networks for a joint marketplace. Thus, the last step signalled the willingness to co-operate with competitors in non-strategic areas if efficiency gains and shareholder value could be generated.

However, there was never a clear move from hierarchical organisations to network organisations. Networks just supplemented the existing organisation either to outsource non-strategic elements or to provide specific elements of a product or service in a more efficient manner.

With the rise of the Internet and the concurrent advent of almost free communication and exchange of information certain industries showed signs of dismal fit of hierarchies for organising in this unprecedented context. What we are starting to see is that different elements of new value chains display different economics, skill sets, and so on, forcing them to think and subsequently organise along new organisational boundaries. And contrary to the old hierarchies, supplementing their organisations with networks of, for example, suppliers to offer a better or cheaper product, the new value chains do not start with existing organisations and their capabilities, but rather with market opportunities. On the basis of these opportunities, products and services are designed and the necessary web of value providers is assembled. For example, Yahoo.com, a well branded search engine defined a new service on the Internet, for which the firm provides the customer relationship management. Yahoo builds the brand, the trust, formalises the customer requirements, and continuously modifies its understanding of customer needs. Yet, in order to truly fulfil customer needs, it needs more than just the customer interface: it requires a certain technology and content as well as the possibility of customers to gain access. In our example, the technology to make Yahoo's ideas of customer needs work is provided by Google, while the required infrastructure to facilitate access is provided by Internet service providers (ISP) and telecommunication companies such as AT&T or Deutsche Telekom.

The lesson to be learned here is that in certain industries and communities, customer needs drive the creation of new value chains. Skills and capabilities are assembled based upon consumer demand, rather than a pre-fabricated product idea.

Our strategy web suggests the following scoring model for this category on our four axes.

On the first axis, *customer centricity*, we find the largest gain as typically hierarchical organisations were set up to fabricate certain products. Networks then began assembling more than just products, that is add-on services. Yet, the new value chains emerging are organised along the needs of their customers and market demands. *Value metrics:* as a measurement to capital markets organisational structures are at best a secondary item. And as not many traditional firms have undergone a transformation into a clicks-and-mortar form, not much can be said about market attributed value add. At the end of the day though, value-based networks will be the better value creator due to their more efficient and effective value handling. *Technology:* as this is a purely organisational issue, much of a change scoring would be undue. One can assert, however, that the change from hierarchy to value networks was only made possible through technological advances; in the end for this case though scoring is of no use. *Organisational configuration* is the main thread of this issue. Developments towards fluid and mobile organisation forms are the key here. The Internet itself is an ubiquitous network of information exchange and value creation. Moreover, many corporate actors in cyberspace display network-based structures of lateral and hori-

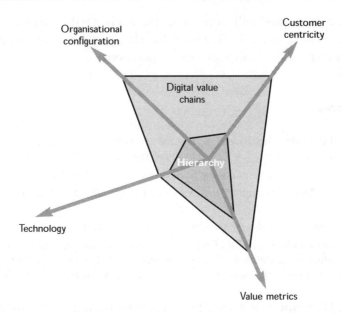

Figure 1.7   From hierarchies to networks and digital value chains

zontal linkages within and among firms. This combination of network structure and digital business design seems to be an appropriate way to cope with the core organisational challenges of the New Economy: speed, flexibility, and focus (Slywotzky and Morrison, 1999). Figure 1.7 summarises the development from hierarchies of the Old Economy era to digital value chains in the New Economy.

Summary

This chapter started with a definitional overview of the Digital Economy and further elaborated on the major patterns of interest in the Digital Economy. A delineation of these digital laws led to the contrasting of changes between the Old and the New Economy. From these differences we derived the challenges ahead and abstracted these into a framework of understanding, called the strategy web. The strategy web helps us understand current developments in the context of the larger picture. To illustrate the individual four axes of the strategy web, a number of trends were used to show the operationalisation of the strategy web and the subsequent implications for organisations.

The next chapter will concretise these changed assumptions in a dynamic context and will illuminate the changing facets of competition, and their respective implications for corporations.

References

Aldrich, D.F. (1999) *Mastering the Digital Marketplace: Practical Strategies for Competitiveness in the New Economy*. New York: John Wiley & Sons.

Coase, R.H. (1937) The nature of the firm. *Economica*, **4**: 386–405.

Kehoe, C.F. (2000) M-commerce: Advantage, Europe. *The McKinsey Quarterly*, **2**: 43–5.

Kelly, K. (1998) *New Rules for the New Economy*. New York: Viking Press.

Kling, R. and Lamb, R. (2000) IT and organizational change in digital economies: a socio-technical approach. In E. Brynjolfsson and B. Kahin (eds), *Understanding the Digital Economy: Data, Tools, and Research*. Cambridge, MA: MIT Press, pp. 295–324.

Marshall, J.F., Christner, R.S. and Almasy, E. (1999) The real point of going digital. *Mercer Management Journal*, (11): 37–48.

Orlikowski, W.J. and Iacono, C.S. (2000) The truth is not out there: an enacted view of the 'digital economy'. In E. Brynjolfsson and B. Kahin (eds), *Understanding the Digital Economy: Data, Tools, and Research*. Cambridge, MA: MIT Press, pp. 352–80.

Shapiro, C. and Varian, H.R. (1999) *Information Rules: A Strategic Guide to the Network Economy*. Boston, MA: Harvard Business School Press.

Siebel, T.M. and House, P. (1999) *Cyber Rules: Strategies for Excelling at e-business*. New York: Random House.

Slywotzky, A.J. and Morrison, D.J. (1999) *Profit Patterns: 30 Ways to Anticipate and Profit from Strategic Forces Reshaping Your Business*. New York: Times Business.

Utterback, J.M. (1994) *Mastering the Dynamics of Innovation: How Companies can Seize Opportunities in the Face of Technological Change*. Boston, MA: Harvard Business School Press.

Woodall, P. (2000) Untangling e-conomics. *The Economist*, **356**(8189): 5–44.

Zerdick, A., Picot, A., Schrape, K. and Artopé, A. (1999) *Die Internet-Ökonomie: Strategien für die digitale Wirtschaft*, 2nd edn. Berlin: Springer-Verlag.

Shift in Competition

CHAPTER CONTENTS

The previous chapter brought up some of the more recent strands surrounding the Internet hype, and discussed them systematically along the lines of our strategy web. Utilising our strategy web allowed us to position this discussion in terms of the origins of the issue, as well as the development and competitive positioning of these issues.

Chapter 2 will further focus the strategy themes by introducing the topic of competition. The nature of capitalist-based systems rests on the foundations of the market efficiency assumptions, which typically are a function of competition and competitive behaviour.

Therefore, the importance of competition also remains a central thrust in the Digital Economy. With the digitalisation of information, drivers of competition and even behaviour, traditional parameters of competition became obsolete. For example, information about products and so on is being placed on the Internet, often in real-time and mostly for free, increasing transparency tremendously. The specificity of assets for production of goods becomes increasingly negligible, as customers can demand highly specified and customised products. And suddenly, intangible assets, such as customer intimacy and customer knowledge, become a differentiating advantage. And in addition to the traditional competitive behaviour, new sense has to be made of a new mode – co-opetition, that is, the combination of competitive and co-operative behaviour. The questions are first to systematise these developments and second to group them accordingly, so that, third, a meaningful strategic direction can be chosen.

The chapter is split into three parts, namely the first section which deals with the drivers of competition (identifying and systematising the issues), the second section focusing on the output of the new competition and the third section which (re-)integrates these discussions into our strategy web concept.

Drivers of competition

We suggest the following four classes of drivers of competition to be helpful in conceiving Digital Economy market mechanisms; they are by no means exhaustive, yet based on our empirical work with start-ups and traditional companies, they seem to represent the key drivers characterising competition and competitive behaviour. One may view them as drivers of competitive behaviour:

1. Speed
2. Efficiency
3. Value of information
4. War for talent.

Speed

When surveying players in the Digital Economy, a number of diverging phenomena with regard to competition and competitive behaviour can be observed. Whether looking at management styles or product innovation cycles one can see the tremendous value derived from speed. We see vastly inexperienced start-up entrepreneurs having no or very little business experience, yet who try to surpass competition merely by their levels of energy and speed. They have no behavioural routines to fall back on, yet they try anyway. And it is their ability to rise and fall, to try, fail and re-try, that has characterised a number of these young entrepreneurs and entrepreneurial companies. Many times this attitude has enabled the creation and growth of a company, the risk for which was often covered by business angels or venture capitalists.

Our central argument for the importance of speed here is that regardless of the faulty business logic – inexperience will lead to failure – we have seen a great many companies succeeding, suggesting that in arenas of competition with few or no entry barriers, the mere application of speed can compensate for the lack of other capabilities. The above example showed the lack of experience being compensated by speed, other exemplars, for instance in the area of product innovation, are conceivable. Moreover, the Internet increases the speed of implementation. Entire processes are being reinvented around the Internet within months. The company Hanes, for example, has copied the Internet-based supply chain management system of its competitor Fruit of the Loom within a six-month period (Mougayar, 1998).

Now, some might argue that speed has always been a key strategic factor, and while that is absolutely true, one must understand that with many traditional hurdles, including asset specificity, entry barriers, information availability, lack of transparency now being reduced to marginal importance, the management of speed is being elevated to a key ability. The message of speed is of course relevant to all companies, yet most pureplay Internet companies were founded on that basis, therefore this imperative holds true mostly for the existing major corporations. These bricks-and-mortar firms are the entities that need to take the imperative of speed to heart. Speed in their processes, speed in the innovation capabilities, but overarching they must aim to make sure that speed becomes part of their organisational culture and philosophy. As always this attitude needs to be credibly lived by the executive management, in order to generate sufficient organisational buy-in and facilitate the necessary trickle-down effects.

Efficiency

The second driver of competition is what many people have called the central benefit of Internet-based electronic commerce. Many processes from mere inquiries to complex auctions can be easily conducted via the Internet, without being constrained by time or location. For many corporate buyers a greater universe of offerings has been made available at no additional cost. Remote suppliers are able to extend their reach and thus their potential customer base. At the same time, this has also limited a company's ability to, for example, offer products over the Internet, yet charge regionally differing prices.

Spill-over efficiency gains were also made possible within companies. Once, for example, an electronic catalogue and content had been decided on for purchasing on the Internet, products to be ordered could be identified unanimously across the organisation. Also, hierarchical routines for ordering now could be depicted in such an electronic catalogue, therefore eliminating the time-consuming paper-based authorisation methods, and hopefully in the process reducing the number of required steps as well.

Efficiency as a driver of competition remains one of the most concrete yet critical elements of Internet-enabled digital commerce. Realising efficiency gains is not a long-term differentiating competitive advantage, rather it is a necessary hygiene criterion with which all companies will have to comply. Companies that fail to take advantage of these efficiency improvements signal clearly to the markets their ineptness for competing in the Digital Economy.

Currently, companies can realise efficiency gains on the procurement side through participation in electronic marketplaces, installation of electronic catalogues and so on. On the sales side, complementing traditional sales channels with Internet channels is a possibility. In addition, many tools and processes for nurturing your customer relationship have been made available. Finally, corporations competing in the New Economy might focus on building up a digital value chain which connects suppliers, buyers, and partner firms in a seamless and efficient way. The IT-enabled flow of information to all members in the value chain makes it possible to aim at near-zero lead times, synchronisation of operations with true customer demand, and immediate response to changes (Aldrich, 1999). A well-known example of a digital value chain is Dell's direct business model, which compresses both time-to-market and order-to-delivery cycles leading to tremendous efficiency gains.

Value of information

With the first driver of competition we discussed the general (perceived) trend of increasing speed of competition and its implications for a firm in terms of organising business activities as well as of reacting to market changes and customer needs. With the second driver of competition we discussed the importance of Internet-induced efficiency gains. The third driver of competition is like efficiency gains, inherently connected with the emergence of the Internet.

The Internet enables private and commercial entities to post any kind of information, which is accessible to everyone. This facility was used early on by companies, for example, to post information about the company, its products and services. Over time, transaction and interaction facilities were added.

Yet, the main characteristic of posting information still brings great value to people and companies alike. The inherently great value for the user is that most information is available near-real-time and for free. For example, newspapers offer content from their print editions in an on-line format, sometimes versioning the content (that is, basic content is for free, extensive political analysis costs per article, and so on) but mostly for free. In other instances, what is core business for one company is a sales tool for another company, which in the end really supports the customer searching for information.

Take the example of a customer requiring information about the state of the art of procurement systems. In a first step the customer may visit the homepages of product vendors such as Ariba or CommerceOne, where useful information about the particular products can be found and often outsourced commissioned white papers, which are intended to provide a more product-neutral view on developments. In a second step, the home-pages of commercial research firms such as Forrester Research, Gartner Group or Yankee Group may be visited. On these sites information about the availability of such information is available and usually abstracts or executive summaries of the reports in question are available for free, yet the full report will cost. Sometimes older report versions are available for free. In any case, the core competence of Forrester Research is commer-cial research and they will therefore charge you for providing a profes-sional report. Or, the customer may be checking the latest available research from the investment banks. Upon entering, for example, the Morgan Stanley Dean Witter (MSDW) homepage he might find a recent report on the issue of concern: electronic procurement. Thus, the potential buyer can get very valuable information from sources for which this particular information is a secondary offering. In this case, MSDW use the research report to show credibility in the area and attract customers for their investment services. This case shows (a) how a customer may find first rate information at close to zero cost, and (b) how similar information may be available at different cost, induced through the fact that research reports are not a core product for MSDW, while they are the main revenue driver for Forrester Research.

At the same time, the rise of virtual consumer-to-consumer communi-ties reorders the relationship between companies and their customers, as vendor- and advertiser-independent information is aggregated and dissem-inated among community members in a timely and cost-efficient way. Community members have the ability to share common interests, relevant information, and comparative purchase experiences. As a result, market transparency increases tremendously, and customers, armed with a growing amount of information, can search out vendors offering the best combination of quality and price. Thus, corporations might increasingly be forced to differentiate through tailored pre- and after-sales services as well as through rapid reactions to customer needs. Another emerging community model whose focal point is information may be termed the expert-to-consumer or the expert-to-business model: the members of communities such as coolQuestion.com can post specific questions that are answered by other community members according to a reverse auction bid. In the near future, we might see professional, highly focused commu-nities in which complex business problems are being solved by leading experts in the field.

War for talent

A last rather important shift in competitive behaviour is the increasing importance of skilled human resources as they are becoming one of the major competitive advantages. In times of rapidly and vastly available amounts of risk capital, superior ideas have no problem receiving funding. With this surge of adequate funding came the drain of young, well-educated professionals who left the carefully drafted consulting and corporate careers for a change to be part of a larger entrepreneurial culture. A culture whose financial rewarding system added up mostly to a bet on the future, that is, options or shares of the company to be founded.

Of course, the wealth to be attained was greatly in excess of the possibilities in traditional careers, yet so were the risks of success and failure. Obviously, monetary incentives were one thing that lured talent to the start-ups, but of equal importance was the desire to become a vital part of a young, rapidly growing organisation, that is, to really see what a difference a single individual's input could make.

So far, the traditional companies remain baffled and merely play the angst card, suggesting that most of the talent will be happily returning once their ventures fail. Surely, many of the ventures will fail and some of the young, professional talent will return, but something grander is happening: a culture shift in the value system and expectations of young professionals. And oddly enough the traditional players have yet to find a potent cure, despite the fact that it can be found within their own organisational genes. And although there is no right answer, it would not seem too far fetched to suggest a feasible way forward which would possibly include a structure consisting of more self-contained smaller units, where seniority is not the criterion for responsibility but rather quality of input. This could be paired financially with an options-type approach, that is, unit-performance based.

Two notes of caution: first, existing organisations consist not only of highly skilled, risk-taking professionals; one has to consider long-serving employees as well, assuming the company still requires these resources. Second, many organisations in the past have made attempts to emulate at least parts of the aforementioned models: to no avail. Mainly because they were not daring and radical enough in their attempts to re-align their human resources policy. For example, many consultancies are going to great pains, through for example building up incubator or accelerator service units, to attract Internet-savvy professionals, yet these new units are being run in much the same way that the traditional consulting business is organised. Therefore, on the one hand, attempts are being made to emulate start-up culture, yet, on the other hand, traditional hierarchy and 'old' evaluation methods prevail. These conflicting messages will ultimately self-destruct these efforts.

We have touched briefly upon the notion of human resource scarcity and the rather recent changes in employee receptivity and motivation. For many traditional firms there is still a long way to go in order to be able to attract the talent they require to compete in the Digital Economy.

One issue that logically follows the initial recruitment of talent is the retaining of such talent. In some areas of the Digital Economy, we have seen trends that prescribe to changing jobs at least every 8–12 months. This is taking the benefits of virtual offices to a limit and, particularly for complex organisations, it cannot be a desirable state. Yet, firms have to contemplate on what mechanisms they want to implement that will help not only to recruit but also to retain the required talent. From the examples cited, we understand that this is a rather complex issue which cannot be solved by simply dishing out share or option packages. Depending on the goal the company wants to achieve, the firm might, in addition, have to implement, for example, a yearly work hour input schedule, allowing the person to spread his work and the subsequent free time. Or, executives being routed around the company on the basis of two- to three-year tasks might be given one assignment off to do whatever they like. Again, we already see this happening occasionally, although most companies fail to deal with the issue systematically. If one accepts the rising importance of human resources as one of the deciding competitive factors, more systematic and top-management attention needs to be paid to the fight for attracting and retaining talent.

In the ensuing sections of this chapter, we will make suggestions on how to incorporate these conceptions of competitive behaviour, that is, speed, efficiency, value of information, and war for talent, into the four elements of a digital competitive landscape. In addition, we present in Chapter 3 our e-roadmapping index (eRI) which is a systemic and holistic mechanism designed to help implement concrete metrics. Thus, for example, to measure a company's ability to 'live' speed, we suggest a six-step 'time-to-x' approach. One 'time-to-x' measurement is time-to-brand which can be used as an internal or external benchmark to assess a firm's branding efforts.

Competitive output: digital landscape

In the first section of this chapter, we described some trends in regard to competitive behaviour and settled on detailing four in particular. These competitive forces are exerting their impact on all organisational entities, regardless of size and location. In this section, we will translate some of these drivers of competition into two scenarios of organisational consequences and subsequently into two ways of strategising from these consequences.

Utilising the competitive factors of speed, efficiency, information availability and human resources scarcity as the determining drivers of competition, we found the following two scenarios to be very helpful in illustrating what the change in competitive behaviour in the Digital Economy means for organisations.

Organisational consequences

Organisational boundaries

Traditionally, organisations were described in terms of a structure that defined roles and rules within an organisation. Anything outside of these structures was seen as a separate entity. Paired with the value chain metaphor it can be used to describe which value-generating activity is carried out within the organisation or outside of it. The economic rationale for quite some time for deciding which activity is carried out inside an organisation has been decided upon the relative cost advantage of inside vs. outside value creation. Based on the work of Coase,[1] this mechanism can be formalised as a decision on the relative cost of conducting transactions.

The aforementioned driver of competition efficiency resembles this mechanism best. Yet, with the advent of easy and cheap communication, we have seen the rise of teleworking, freelancing, project-based teams, and even virtual teams. Usually these phenomena are cited to suggest that the traditional boundaries of organisations do dissolve. In fact, these elements are mostly just divergent models of organising inhouse activities. And typically, when outside people are brought in for freelancing work, the work in question is hardly at the heart of an organisation's core value proposition. Other forms of co-operation or addition of outside experience, for example with consultant firms, is usually performed on non-central value-generating activities.

However, the Digital Economy does enforce its pressures on organisational boundaries, for example, the issue of speed has led many traditional firms to separate their electronic commerce activities into stand-alone entities. And while there is an ongoing debate on whether dot-corp or dot-com is the better form of organisation (that is, incubating electronic commerce activities inhouse vs. outside the boundaries of the firm), separation of electronic commerce activities from the existing firm, does resemble in many ways the portfolio holdings of traditional venture capitalists, although admittedly the governance mechanisms and degree of ownership may vary.

This signifies substantial differences in the degree of a distinct boundary and therefore forces existing firms to think about mechanisms whereby the benefits of separating electronic commerce activities can be reaped and be reintegrated into the learning and innovation capabilities of the grand organisation. Most executives today have garnered the benefits of harvesting dotcom activities and are eagerly spinning off mature units to collect the stock market benefits, yet they fail to look ahead to see what these separated units could do for the central value-generating activity of the firm.

The assumption is that sensible value-generating activity might well be pushed outside of the traditional boundaries of an organisation, but that in order to obtain the full monetary and knowledge benefits, mechanisms need to be designed that could create not just a one-way but a spiralling, interactive connection between the two entities.

Another example to show the implication of blurring boundary definitions is the war for talent. For some time, firms have outsourced non-core activities and in times of peak demand even more central functions. Yet, most firms realise that a number of key personnel may no longer want to be bound into the confines of a lifetime employment contract, but look for more freedom which could be found, for example, in freelancing contracts. So the tide it seems has turned from companies refusing to offer lifetime employment, to employees refusing long-term commitments. In many ways, existing models of co-operation are rather binary: you either work for us or you do not.

Many employees have been able to turn that pressure around. Rather than receiving this information as a threat, this could be a good opportunity for many firms to revisit their employment models, and more importantly their founding philosophy or basic principles. Just reducing the issue to supply and demand, and therefore scarcity of skilled resources, seems a bit too simple.

The opportunity for the firm is to establish a common language for all and for anyone wishing to work in and around the firm's core activity. Defining the various value-creating activities is the first step, followed by a second step defining various layers of commitment and a third defining clear roles of activity/engagement. This construct is then connected with a clear reward system which is coupled with a measurable achievement system.

Many professional services firms today are trying to operate in such a manner, but usually just define an area of expertise and a resource allocation system, which is coupled with a performance-based system. Yet, these systems lack a common ground and have very little understanding of commitment. Most importantly, these systems typically just exploit resources, leading to easily predictable time intervals of brain drain, which is just a consequence of high burnout rates. While this model is acceptable in small niches which are defined by high supply rates and high financial rewards, larger firms cannot afford to operate in such a mode for a long period of time.

Thus, in this example, firms may take the opportunity of blurring organisational boundaries to:

1. Re-define their common principles
2. Define the various value-creation activities
3. Separate various layers of commitment
4. Establish a system of rewards based on achievement of pre-defined goals
5. Continuously nourish the skills and competencies required.

This action plan should enable the firm to re-focus their core value creation activities and to define the skills required for the variety of business processes, paired with models of co-operation that will facilitate the demands of many classes of employees while giving the firm clear indications of achievement and commitment.

Organisations as complex adaptive systems

The second organisational consequence we found worth while discussing is that of organisations resembling complex adaptive systems rather than linear progressions. Even when considering only the diversity of the four initial elements, speed, efficiency, value of information, and war for talent, we realise that these concepts signify complexity – complexity that cannot be reduced to, for example, progressing steps on a continuum. Evolutionary biologists have used the term complex adaptive system for some time to describe how even the smallest biological entities and populations are inter-dependent and evolve over time.

The point of reference here is not so much the biological metaphor, but more the understanding that viewing organisations as complex systems might enhance our ability to strategise.

The basic assumption from a systems perspective is that very few events can be understood from a linear and causal point of view. This requires top management to visualise the 'larger picture', a picture that cannot be fully understood by measuring just past internal and external performance. Despite our knowledge that the past is a poor proxy for future predictions, many executives act differently. And while, of course, the psychological need for certainty can be understood, neglecting the realities and using predictions based on history is a dismal strategy for leading an organisation to future success.

What needs to be done instead is to instil *restlessness* in organisations, therefore reducing complacency and inertia. In addition, *diversity* in all dimensions would seem a valuable source of future fitness, as it counters our intuitive reaction of inbreeding. Restlessness and diversity are to serve as inputs to strategic management that starts with a good understanding of the organisation's 'imprinted genes' – to stay with the biologists' metaphor – and from there on use multiple venues to search for future strategic peaks. The drivers of competition are fairly simple, yet may require substantial cultural change, the mirror on the organisation's genes can also be facilitated. What is needed next are the dimensions for plotting the firm's own strengths and the search for the way forward. Naturally, we believe that our strategy grid provides the required dimensions. In the first step, we use the e-roadmapping web to plot the firm's current capabilities and in a second step we add the factor time and draw the four dimensions so that progressions can be displayed.

Examples of firms having instilled restlessness and diversity can be found in many existing corporations which, for example, assume that a certain percentage of sales in two or three years has to come from products not invented yet. Diversity can be fostered by continuous job rotation, periodical team mixing or filling positions to a certain percentage with outsiders.

The prime example of a company that has instilled these cultural values, that has reflected on its strengths and that has plotted (and pursued) multiple parallel strategies in a competitive environment is surely Microsoft. Yet, a few other Digital Economy players like the German Brokat AG also come to mind.

Microsoft found their strengths in the 1980s to be in the software business. From this starting point they plotted multiple routes into operating system and business applications, therefore hedging their bets.

The Brokat company started in the Internet security business. Today, they also provide security by other (more traditional) means. In addition, Brokat offers integrated solutions, that is, not only security features for banking, but full-blown banking software.

In the previous sections, we discussed two organisational consequences of the Digital Economy. Understanding these scenarios now allows us to visit two strategies we derived from our understanding of these organisational consequences.

Strategies derived from organisational consequences of blurring boundaries and complex systems

In our approach to the changing terms of competition, we first analysed the most prevalent four drivers of competition, which in and by themselves constitute little meaning. In a second step, some of these factors were used to create organisational concepts of certain tendencies with which companies today are faced. Yet, these facets of digital landscapes do nothing but exert their influence on firms and it is now in this third step that we want to show in an exemplary manner, how organisations can actually use the competitive factors to turn them into viable strategic options.

Diagonalisation of value creation is one of the strategies that firms can devise to cope with some of the drivers of competition and organisational consequences of the Digital Economy. We define diagonalisation as the firm's ability to take an internal value chain or value-generating activity and make it available with marginal to zero cost to existing or potential customers for purposes of customer acquisition or retention outside of the core business of the firm in question, and for the greater benefit of all parties involved.

For example, assume a telecommunication company has decided to cut their cost of indirect spending by standardising processes and items through the implementation of an electronic procurement solution. A typical electronic procurement solution today, from for example the likes of Ariba, will depict a whole company purchasing policy through the application of a software tool. Utilisation of such tools will bring about bundling effects and therefore drive down unit prices, but more importantly, will bring down the average process cost by up to 80 per cent. For the majority of indirect spend these savings on process cost will be the main target of such initiatives.

Diagonalisation now would call the company to use the existing electronic procurement application for the purpose of acquiring and/or retaining customers, for example in their segment of small- and medium-sized enterprises. Using Internet technology the telecommunication company would make available parts or the whole of their electronic product catalogue through an extranet-based system to these customers.

Using such a system would bring benefits to all parties involved. The telecommunication firm attracts and/or retains customers at virtually no additional cost, in addition to exploiting even larger volume bundling effects. The actual suppliers of goods attain extra sales, that is, extend an existing sales channel, also at no additional cost. The customer receives a value-added service at no extra charge, enabling him or her to optimise the purchasing processes, in addition to realising unit prices usually not feasible in a stand-alone situation.

The deployment of such strategy, as shown, incurs literally no cost for any party involved and just generates greater benefit for all participants. Any firm may use the above definition of diagonalisation to scan for such opportunities. And certainly this strategy is not covered by what we currently would conceive as vertical or horizontal integration strategies.

Of course, one needs to be cautious as to the potential of this strategy. First, not even the most digitised of companies will find too many applications feasible for such strategising efforts. And second, in this situation particularly, the first movers will be able to realise most of the benefits of such diagonalisation. Nonetheless, diagonalisation is a fairly simple strategy for reaping some benefits of these changing terms of competition.

Rugged landscape strategising is the second possibility of proactively using the changing terms of competition. This approach to strategising is based on the four dimensions of our e-roadmapping method. Plotting one's own competitive strength on the e-roadmap is the starting point (and first characteristic) for our rugged landscape strategising.

The necessary pre-condition of restlessness and diversity was already elaborated on in our previous section on managing complex adaptive systems.

Plotting the status quo reveals a company's position of relative competitive advantage. Using this as the starting point, the objective of the forward looking journey is to approximate the next strategic peaks and valleys. We use peak as a metaphor here for a future strategic opportunity, characterised, for example, by high profit margins or sustainable competitive advantages. Valleys of course are the logical counterpart.

Through applying knowledge of the company's own strengths it is now necessary to embark on an exercise characterised by the following two elements:

- Extending existing value opportunities vs. destructive creation opportunities
- Multiple routing.

The first exercise element focuses on the horizon of the strategic search. In a first instance the near-term opportunities, or close-by peaks need to be discovered. These opportunities will in many cases be closely related to existing capabilities of the firm.

The second exercise element focuses on the more distant strategic future, a future that may be based on current capabilities, yet it may consist of competencies that are currently not within a firm's array of central capabilities. In metaphoric language, one may conceive of the first element as the two-hour hiking trip, while the second signifies the first ascent of the Himalayas. Both explorative elements are necessary to give the firm a chance at being competitive in the future, however, the mix of both elements will vary greatly depending on the industry.

The second characteristic of rugged landscape strategising is the necessity to provide for searches of multiple routes. Understanding one's own strength does not reduce a firm to a single capability. Rather it requires the firm to use these capabilities as the starting point for multiple, even counter-directional searches. There is no golden rule as to how many directions need to be examined, yet exploring at least one direction of each of the four e-roadmapping dimensions (technology, value metrics, transformation, and customers) seems fairly sensible.

Applying rugged landscape strategising will allow the company to be in a constant search in multiple directions for near-term and long-term strategic opportunities.

An example of such a rugged landscape strategising effort may again be taken from a telecommunication firm. The firm applied the e-roadmapping dimensions to find out that their most valuable asset is their regional groundedness. On the basis of this capability, searches in the directions of the four e-roadmapping dimensions were started, coupled with a take on near-term opportunities and distant, destructive creation opportunities. The firm, for example, found as a near-term technological opportunity that most of the smaller enterprises had fairly costly access to the Internet. Taking their knowledge of customer behaviour from the core telephone activity, the company bundled traditional phone services with a broadband Internet access, opening a profit opportunity of a few months in relation to the competing telecommunication companies and infrastructure service providers.

In the more distant view, the company found on their search indications that the media for accessing telecommunication services would slowly converge, giving the producers of convergence hardware a central position. This led the company to invest through acquisition activities, enabling it to push actively towards designing and manufacturing such product.

Summary

The purpose of this chapter was to show some exemplary factors of the changing terms of competition. The intention was not so much to present the reader with a laundry list, but more importantly, with a detailed context on these selected exemplary factors and drivers of competition.

In a second step, we aggregated these changing terms of competition to a couple of scenarios exerting their influence on firms as organisational consequences, or put differently, as a distinct changing context. Adding context allows the reader a more thorough understanding of how deeply the Digital Economy can influence organisations.

In the third and last step of the chapter, we introduced two selected strategies which are based on our e-roadmapping concept and the pre-requisite of cultural values of organisational restlessness and diversity. The diagonalisation example showed very concretely how existing applications can be used with little effort for the purpose of defying competition and generating substantial competitive advantage. The second strategy laid down our more conceptual thinking on a process for systematically assuring that a company actively and continuously searches its competitive landscape for near- and long-term opportunities of varying direction.

Notes

1. cf. our discussion in Chapter 1 on digital laws

References

Aldrich, D.F. (1999) *Mastering the Digital Marketplace: Practical Strategies for Competitiveness in the New Economy*. New York: John Wiley & Sons.

Mougayar, W. (1998) *Opening Digital Markets: Battle Plans and Business Strategies for Internet Commerce*. New York: McGraw-Hill.

CHAPTER 3

Strategising in the Digital Economy: e-roadmapping

STRATEGISING IN THE DIGITAL ECONOMY: E-ROADMAPPING

In the first chapter of this book, we introduced the four dimensions – *customer centricity*, *value metrics*, *technology*, and *organisational configuration* – for conceptualising a firm's position in the digital context. The second chapter depicted the changing terms of competition in the New Economy and the implications for corporate strategy. In this chapter, the e-roadmapping methodology which intends to make comprehensive sense of the challenges and opportunities that arise in the New Economy will be introduced: e-roadmapping is a tool to analyse the specific situation of a company in the digital environment and to design a strategic roadmap to the digital landscape. The e-roadmapping process is divided into three parts, namely the analysis part, the design part, and the actual e-roadmap, that is, the end-product. Figure 3.1 provides an overview of the e-roadmapping process. Subsequently, the three building blocks – analysis, design, and end-product – will be displayed in detail.

Analysis

The analysis section is divided into the strategy, resources and technology and the portfolio part. The *strategy, resources* and *technology analysis*

Analysis		Design		End-product
Strategy, resources and technology	Portfolio	Community and competition	Strategy design	e-roadmap
■ Identify the currently used business strategies ■ Map the product strategy portfolio and portfolio of customers ■ Delineate functional organisation structure and resources ■ Map the competitive environment ■ Identify the relevant processes and the existing technologies	■ Determine the resulting central competencies ■ Unbundle competencies according to value chain elements/ processes ■ Map unbundled competencies with key skills	■ Define the (new) community ■ Map the new competitive environment ■ Identify possible benchmarks	■ Design multiple digital strategies ■ Determine the landscape and relevant boundaries ■ Map the 'strategy web' (portfolio of possible strategies)	■ Develop portfolio of strategic options ■ Identify paths on how to achieve 'strategy web' ■ Define pertinent value metrics and profit models

Figure 3.1   The e-roadmapping process

seeks to concretise the currently employed strategies and to map them according to the product strategy portfolio. It further outlines the existing organisational structure along with a plot of the customer portfolio and the competition. In addition, the available (and utilised) technology along with the critical and relevant processes are identified. Key to this analysis part is the systemic understanding of the existing organisation, which is facilitated through the utilisation of the traditional value chain approach. This exercise is necessary to understand better the currently selected business strategies in the context of the existing customer segmentation and the underlying business processes. The task should also help the organisation to reflect on its core capabilities, which will be the basis for the further digital strategising process.

The second part of the analysis uses the concretised understanding to unbundle the organisational elements into central competencies of the existing organisation according to the existing value chain processes. This *portfolio analysis* is completed by mapping the unbundled competencies with the required skills. This part is necessary to take the self-reflected organisational strengths and aggregate these into distinguishable competencies. With the specific descriptions of these competencies, one can subsequently determine which key human resources and technical skills are required to meaningfully display this core strength.

Design

The design section consists of the community and competition and the strategy design part. The *community and competition part* defines the new community of co-opetition, plots the respective players and/or competitors, and seeks to define the possible benchmarks. This level entails questioning the assumptions of traditional competition and subsequently defining a new community of competition. As an end result, for example, a traditional car manufacturer may find itself not competing solely against other car companies, but in the arena of other mobility providers. In the *strategy design part*, the digital context is determined and the possible strategies, along with the respective limitations, can be generated. The strategy design entails understanding a company's strengths (the starting point), being aware of all competing players (the context), and defining multiple yet complementary routes to the next strategy 'peak' (the direction).

How can this new community of co-opetition be found? The suggestion is that, only through major shifts in assumptions on what constitutes strategic value and digital strategising, can an answer be found. Figure 3.2 visualises how established models of the Old Economy era should be supplemented by new approaches of the digital age. It goes without saying that the traditional concepts are still valid today and will also be of importance for business practice in the future. Nonetheless, corporations need to comprehend and to integrate new approaches to strategising in order to remain competitive in the digital age. In the following, the four axes and the entailed concepts will be depicted in detail.

On the horizontal axis, the *operational efficiency* dimension entails established approaches such as cost cutting, process reengineering, and revenue enhancements, all of which maintain importance yet fail to give a sustainable differentiating advantage. New strategic value can be created by (a) generating rapid time-to-market cycles and (b) combining speed with the ability to dominate, that is, the ability quickly to scale the innovation to high market penetration and, ultimately, to achieve market dominance. In addition, new or modified value metrics such as online conversion rates, registered users, speed of implementation, market valuation, and so on need to be integrated into a firm's steering and control

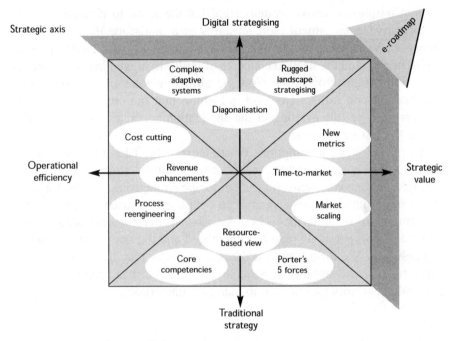

Figure 3.2   e-roadmapping strategic axis

system. This view can be further supplemented with the understanding that these metrics are no longer solely fixed on accounting statements but, more importantly, on the value of options an organisation generates with its intended new digital positioning.

On the *vertical axis*, we find traditional strategy concepts like Porter's five forces, the resource-based view or the core competencies approach. To some extent, these established concepts remain valid in the New Economy, yet they do not provide comprehensive and sufficient guidance for navigating in the unprecedented and fast-changing environment of the digital age. Therefore, we suggest new concepts of digital strategising to find application: complex adaptive systems, rugged landscape strategising, and diagonalisation, which paired with the strategic value drivers generate the e-roadmap. As was exemplified in detail in Chapter 2, these approaches can be conceptualised as follows: first, increasing complexity combined with the further need to constantly adapt, that is, iterative strategising, becomes a key organisational ability. Rugged landscape strategising is the vision and understanding of the value of options of an organisation, that is, starting with a company's central competence, yet venturing out on different venues to master the next challenge through systematic execution. Complex adaptive system signifies the need to conceive of the competitive environment more in terms of a landscape than as a linear function. Visualising the various 'valleys and peaks' of a landscape then helps understand the need to conceive of multiple rugged landscape strategies. Diagonalisation is the strategic ability to take an existing digital application and utilise it in such a fashion that the company incurs no further cost, yet the availing of the application generates sufficient added value to existing customers.

Once the 'new' assumptions of strategic value (that is, new metrics, time-to-market, and market scaling) and of digital strategising (that is, complex adaptive systems, rugged landscape strategising, and diagonalisation) are in place, the new arena of co-opetition – a space of constant flux and fluidity of relations that is best described as iterations between competition and co-operation – can be concretised and the new digital strategies be designed. So, for example, a car manufacturer may have now decided to compete in the mobility provider arena and the task at hand is (a) to plot possible new strategies and (b) to map the competitors.

End-product

On the basis of the four dimensions of our strategy web *customer centricity*, *value metrics*, *technology*, and *organisational configuration*, a corporation's competitive position but also a new portfolio of strategies can be mapped. Particularly, the differentiation to competitors and partners becomes conceptually and visually more clear. That is to say, once the options are generated, feasible paths to achievement need to be outlined and success needs to be measured through implementation of new or modified value metrics and profit models.

In the following section, we provide an outlook of options for utilisation of the e-roadmapping tool in the concrete context of the IT and the automotive industry. The first example shows the e-roadmapping *process* in detail, while the second example focuses on the *content* possibilities of the e-roadmapping tool.

e-roadmapping: a concrete example

To concretise the e-roadmapping tool and process, we will depict in the following the case of a Swiss IT-service company, with whom we conducted an e-roadmapping study earlier this year.

The organisation in question had in the past year successfully completed the implementation of their ERP software and just recently opened their online shop. It had expanded into three adjacent geographies and had over the past years become the market leader in their targeted market segment. The firm's customers were mostly businesses and less than 10 per cent of sales were consumer purchases.

We were confronted with questions pertaining to the range of product offerings and services, further internationalisation and technology-enabled strategic challenges.

To be able to systematise the questions posed, categorisation was done according to the four axes of the strategy web:

Questions pertaining to customer centricity

- Which of the services and products we offer today will our customers require in the future?
- Based on our core competencies, what new products and services will our customers require in the future?
- How should we segment our existing customer base?
- What are the customer needs of tomorrow, around which we should organise our segmentation?
- Are we targeting the right customers?

Questions regarding value metrics

- Are we putting our strategic purchasing position to optimal use?
- What are our options for growth and geographic expansion through leverage of our core skills?
- Are our business options (based on the core skills) sufficiently scalable and competitive in the long run?

Questions pertaining to technology

- How do we maintain certainty of technological fitness, in light of existing ERP and web-front-end investments?
- What further technology will be necessary to realise our business strategies?

Questions regarding organisational configuration

- What are our core skills and competencies?
- What services should be outsourced?
- How should we conceptualise and organise our partner network?

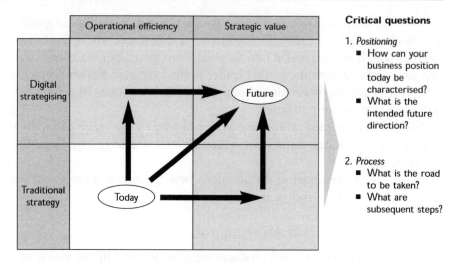

Figure 3.3   Positioning today and in the future

How sustainable is our profit model and what will be the profit sources in the future?

The fundamental questions the company was faced with are illustrated in Figure 3.3.

To help the company to position itself successfully in the Digital Economy, we suggested the following e-roadmapping process:

Phase I: Analysis

Analysis of the existing strategies, resources and technologies (inside analysis)

Determination of the emerging trends, in terms of products, services, geographies, competitors, and technologies (market analysis)

Aggregation of the data into sensible scenarios and alternatives, in terms of central competencies, competitive value chain positions, and competence-mapped key skills through application of the strategy web (analysis portfolio).

Phase II: Design

Definition of the competitive environment through utilisation of the four strategy web axes (customer centricity, value metrics, technology, and organisational configuration)

▦ Decision on new strategy portfolio and subsequent plotting of strategies in the strategy web.

Phase III: End-product

▦ Concretisation of new strategy design
▦ Implementation planning
▦ Definition of new value and performance metrics.

Based on this proposal, we found an agreeable mode of co-operation that saw completion of the study within three months.

In phase Ia, interviews with various layers and functions of the organisation were conducted. For example, account and marketing executives, as well as country executives were interviewed and deep insights into customer structures, geographic subtleties, perceived competencies, and skills were gathered. In addition, country surveys were sent out and completed to gain a systematic understanding, including sales data, product turnover, and so on. For this purpose, specific templates were designed and subsequently filled in with the help of local staff. This way a grounded understanding from planning/forecasting, purchasing to sales and marketing functions was achieved.

This time also served to assemble the project team, consisting of a central core team, and an extended team (country, functional areas).

In parallel (phase Ib), independent desk research was conducted. The result of the market analysis along the dimensions of products, countries, and competition was concentrated into a couple of meta-trends, which further incorporated the applicable e-business trends and technological developments.

The result of phase I is a detailed understanding of existing core value propositions, including technical competencies and human skills as well as a comprehension of applicable meta-trends. This understanding is manifested through the presentation of a rough portfolio of strategy options.

In phase II, the strategy web and the four new dimensions of co-opetition were introduced. The first purpose of the strategy web is to visually depict the possible new configurations for the company based on the results of the internal and external factor analysis of phase I (Figure 3.4).

The options that were generated include the *category portal* (for example, becoming the purchasing gate for certain IT-products), the *back-end integration* (of all supplier, buyer and value-added service processes) and *the value-added service provider strategy* (that is, the real-time integration of various value-added services such as logistics, payment, quality

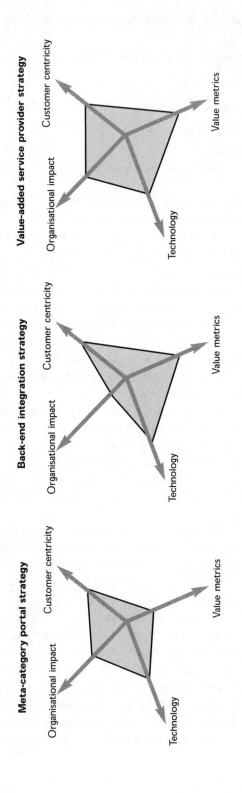

Figure 3.4 Portfolio of strategy webs

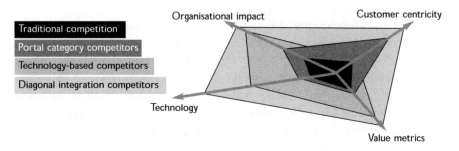

New community of co-opetition

Traditional competition
Portal category competitors
Technology-based competitors
Diagonal integration competitors

Organisational impact

Customer centricity

Technology

Value metrics

Figure 3.5   Community of co-opetition

assurance, and so on). For each of these strategies an 'as is' and a 'future' visual is presented; the delta, that is, the respective distance is the amount of change the company would still have to undergo.

The second purpose of the strategy web is to draw the boundaries of the new area of co-opetition and, subsequently, to plot the community of new competitors. This chart helps to visualise the particular strengths of competitors and specifically how classes of competitors compare. Through the visualisation of the community of co-opetition the efforts necessary to reach the future value position become blatantly clear.

In this particular case, the rough options were presented to the board. In an off-site event, the details of these scenarios were discussed and elaborated on, leading to a decision on which strategic path to follow (Figure 3.5).

In phase III of this project, the elected options were further detailed. This included specifying the required human resource and technology skills, as well as strategic partners to bridge the current delta factor. In addition to the input factor, an implementation roadmap was construed. This strategic positioning paper was then used for the final management decision on which future strategy to embark on.

In this particular case, the strategy work has been completed by now and implementation is on its way. In the specific market segment, it was further found that the timing was superbly ahead of the competition and it is believed that a sustainable value proposition was achieved. The e-roadmapping tool showed how in the Digital Economy strategy work that combines new thinking with systematic work can be completed successfully.

e-roadmapping: an automotive example

The fundamental changes and challenges resulting from the arising Digital Economy are forcing all players (and subsequent elements) of the traditional automotive supply chain to rethink their basic assumptions about customer relationships, competition, and business models. In this fast-changing environment, value leaves economically obsolete business models and flows to new business models that more effectively create value for customers and capture value for producers (Slywotzky, 1996). For this reason, incumbents have to ask themselves what business they are really in and which part of the value creation in the automotive industry they will be able to perform better than current and potential rivals in the digital future.

This section displays future perspectives of the automotive value creation in the truly global, fast-changing, and highly interconnected context of the Digital Economy: first, a comprehensive e-business model for the automotive industry will be provided as an example of an integrated, one-stop value proposition that combines online and offline activities of all relevant stakeholders in the car distribution process. Second, on a macro or community level, our model of the customer-driven network unbundles the supply chain of the automotive industry and reorganises the value-creating activities around customers' needs. The reader may notice that these models cannot yield precise predictions because of the unprecedented and fast-changing nature of the Digital Economy and the enormous variety of different economic, regulatory, social, and temporal contexts of the global automotive industry (Orlikowski and Iacono, 2000). Nonetheless, these models can help understanding of the patterns of change and aim to provide a framework to transform the automotive supply chain into a digital network of value creation and information exchange. It remains to be seen to what extent these ideas will be realised in business practice.

Analysis

As was mentioned earlier, the profound changes induced by the emerging Digital Economy create a new retailing landscape in the automotive industry and present a number of strategic challenges for the incumbent stakeholders. Carmakers and dealers risk losing control of the customer relationship as new intermediaries arise, which empower the consumer by offering compelling content, price transparency, and convenient one-stop shopping solutions. These flexible 'pureplay' competitors are moving at

Internet speed selling bits not atoms. As they do not have to manage and operate cost-intensive physical resources such as assembly lines, ware-houses, distribution centres, and so on, they are able to focus solely on marketing, servicing customer needs, and building the customer relation-ship. Nonetheless, incumbent players of the automotive industry have significant advantages to exploit when they decide to go digital: in-depth market know-how, brand familiarity and trust, physical presence of show-rooms and service facilities as well as long-standing customer knowledge. The challenge is to transform these assets into a digital business design (Marshall et al., 1999).

This leads one to the conclusion that carmakers have a clear need to rapidly define strategies that combine the advantages of online buying and information services with the incumbents' offline assets. The empowered consumer of the Internet age has to be the starting as well as the focal point of these strategies: this consumer obtains a rich amount of informa-tion, expects to get the best price offer, and looks for a convenient one-stop shopping experience (Dudenhöfer, 1999). In order to meet the needs of the empowered customer, carmakers have to integrate other intermedi-aries such as dealers, company showrooms, and so on and complementary partners such as financial services institutions, insurance companies, repair facilities, and so on into their digital strategy. By combining all these different competencies into a holistic and seamless online and offline value proposition, it will be possible to meet customers' needs from the information phase to after-sales services and thus to increase customer retention and customer lifetime value. Figure 3.6 visualises the e-business model for the automotive industry.

The e-business model illustrated in Figure 3.6 shows a one-stop value proposition that combines online and offline activities of all relevant stakeholders in the car distribution process. In this integrated offering, customer support and service traverses the entire vehicle life cycle, from search and information capabilities, to the purchase decision, on through delivery to repair services, and finally to the repeat purchase decision. The objective is to win new customers, to lock-in existing customers, and thus, to maximise the customer lifetime value by providing a primarily web-enabled one-stop source that meets the entire range of customer needs related to the car purchase and its usage. While intermediaries such as dealers, company showrooms, and so on and complementary partners such as financial services institutions, insurance companies, repair facilities, and so on contribute to this holistic value proposition, the car manufac-turer should be the anchor establishing the rules and owning the customer relationship. Nonetheless, despite increasing propensity of consumers to

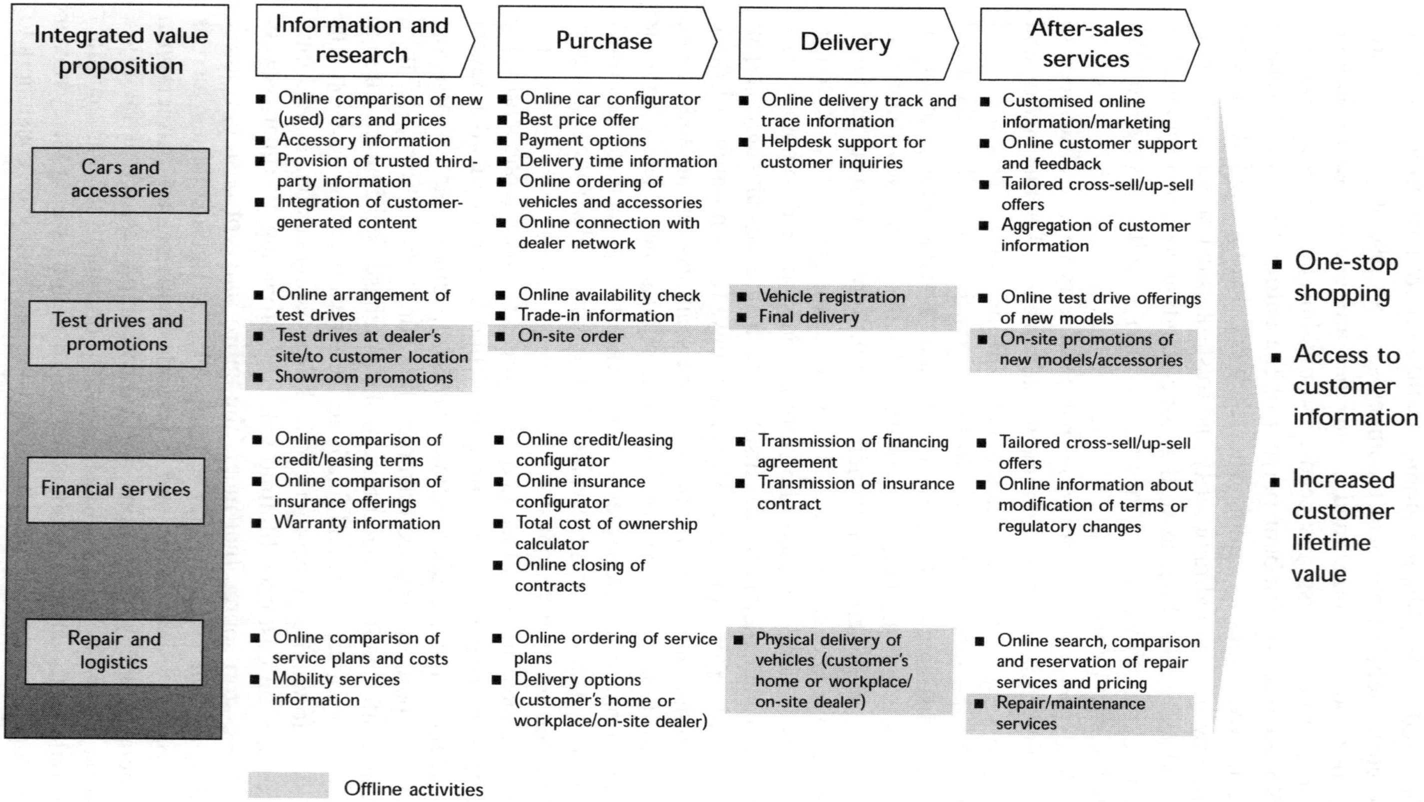

Integrated value proposition

	Information and research	Purchase	Delivery	After-sales services
Cars and accessories	▪ Online comparison of new (used) cars and prices ▪ Accessory information ▪ Provision of trusted third-party information ▪ Integration of customer-generated content	▪ Online car configurator ▪ Best price offer ▪ Payment options ▪ Delivery time information ▪ Online ordering of vehicles and accessories ▪ Online connection with dealer network	▪ Online delivery track and trace information ▪ Helpdesk support for customer inquiries	▪ Customised online information/marketing ▪ Online customer support and feedback ▪ Tailored cross-sell/up-sell offers ▪ Aggregation of customer information
Test drives and promotions	▪ Online arrangement of test drives ▪ Test drives at dealer's site/to customer location ▪ Showroom promotions	▪ Online availability check ▪ Trade-in information ▪ On-site order	▪ Vehicle registration ▪ Final delivery	▪ Online test drive offerings of new models ▪ On-site promotions of new models/accessories
Financial services	▪ Online comparison of credit/leasing terms ▪ Online comparison of insurance offerings ▪ Warranty information	▪ Online credit/leasing configurator ▪ Online insurance configurator ▪ Total cost of ownership calculator ▪ Online closing of contracts	▪ Transmission of financing agreement ▪ Transmission of insurance contract	▪ Tailored cross-sell/up-sell offers ▪ Online information about modification of terms or regulatory changes
Repair and logistics	▪ Online comparison of service plans and costs ▪ Mobility services information	▪ Online ordering of service plans ▪ Delivery options (customer's home or workplace/on-site dealer)	▪ Physical delivery of vehicles (customer's home or workplace/on-site dealer)	▪ Online search, comparison and reservation of repair services and pricing ▪ Repair/maintenance services

- One-stop shopping
- Access to customer information
- Increased customer lifetime value

Offline activities

Figure 3.6 The e-business model for the automotive industry

select and purchase vehicles online, the traditional physical presence of showrooms, customer advisory services as well as maintenance and repair services remains an important source of customer retention and brand building in the automotive industry.

As the anchor of the system, the car manufacturer has to constantly monitor the compliance with quality standards and service levels, the real-time flow of information to all members, and the value-added contribution of all involved parties. Moreover, inherent conflicts of interest in this network, that is, the need to meet consumers' wishes for online car buying with the traditional dealers' business model, have to be balanced by the anchor (A.T. Kearney, 1999). Concerning its own contribution to value creation in the e-business model, the carmaker has to rethink its traditional strategy and has to define its core business processes for the digital age. In the following, the concept of unbundling the traditional value chain and restructuring into a customer-focused network will be presented.

Design

Looking beneath the surface of most traditional companies, three elementary kinds of businesses can be identified (Hagel and Singer, 1999): a customer relationship business, a product innovation business, and an infrastructure business. Each of these businesses is very different concerning their economic, competitive, and cultural imperatives (cf. Figure 3.7). As more and more information exchange and business activities move on to electronic networks, Hagel and Singer (1999) argue that basic assumptions of traditional organisations about their core business will become overturned. As a consequence, highly integrated corporations that keep their core processes bundled together will have significant disadvantages in comparison with new, flexible competitors that are specialists in one of the above-mentioned elementary businesses. Some car manufacturers, for example, may decide – or be forced – to outsource all their manufacturing operations some day to highly focused infrastructure management specialists and to concentrate on product innovation and branding (Hagel and Singer, 1999). Other carmakers may start to move strategically into the after-market taking equity positions or acquiring online car brokers, dealer networks, financial services institutions, and so on (Ealey and Troyano-Bermúdez, 1996, 2000).

In view of the above, it seems reasonable to forecast that the supply chain of the automotive industry will continue to change dramatically. All stakeholders of the automotive supply chain might need to fundamentally

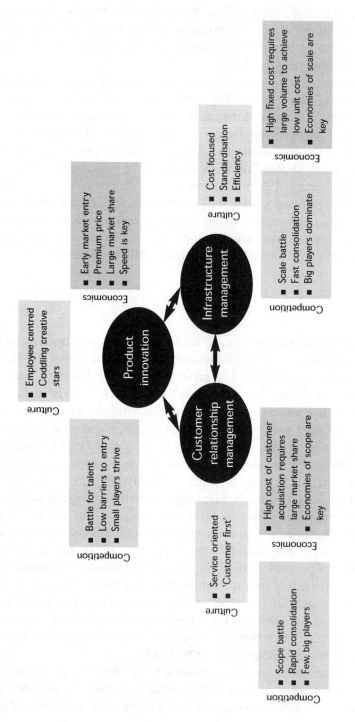

Figure 3.7   Unbundling the traditional organisation
(*Source:* Hagel and Singer, 1999)

Product innovation

Infrastructure management

Customer relationship management

Economics
- Early market entry
- Premium price
- Large market share
- Speed is key

Culture
- Employee centred
- Coddling creative stars

Competition
- Battle for talent
- Low barriers to entry
- Small players thrive

Culture
- Cost focused
- Standardisation
- Efficiency

Economics
- High fixed cost requires large volume to achieve low unit cost
- Economies of scale are key

Competition
- Scale battle
- Fast consolidation
- Big players dominate

Culture
- Service oriented
- 'Customer first'

Economics
- High cost of customer acquisition requires large market share
- Economies of scope are key

Competition
- Scope battle
- Rapid consolidation
- Few, big players

rethink their traditional organisation and might need to redefine their business models for competing in the Digital Economy. Therefore, our model of the customer-driven network provides a glimpse of the future by unbundling the supply chain of the automotive industry and by reorganising the value-creating activities around customers' needs (cf. Figure 3.8). The elements of this customer-focused network are highly specialised, intensely inter-linked, and aim at synchronisation of resources and information flow with true customer demand (Aldrich, 1999). In the future, the automotive supply chain could be organised as a direct business model (cf. Dell's built-to-order model) in which customised demand nearly exactly matches supply and which revolves around a digital order processing, inventory management, and manufacturing system, that removes the assets from an asset-intensive process. Nonetheless, until this scenario becomes reality, there is still a long way to go and many challenges such as the integration of inherent physical elements (for example test drives, delivery, repair services, and so on) into the digital built-to-order model have to be resolved.

Concretising an automotive e-roadmap: mobility provider

A concrete strategic map for a car manufacturer may be the strategic intention of becoming a mobility provider. As a mobility provider, the organisation intends to fulfil any and all mobility needs of consumer or business entities. As such, it is vital to gain a superior access point to the traveller. For purposes of illustration let us assume the case of a business traveller, wanting to depart from his Stuttgart office at 9 a.m. to arrive for a meeting in Hamburg at 1 p.m.

The mobility provider now first needs to gain access to the customer and his specific demand. One may do so through providing a WAP service available to, for example, all Lufthansa Senators (the premium customer segment of the German airline). Thus, the customer can vocalise his requirements. The mobility provider now needs to provide a number of diverging choices, that is, pick-up at address with taxi cab, take-off from airport, pick-up at airport and deliver at destination, services which, by definition, all need to be seamlessly integrated. Once the customer has made his choice (flight vs. train or speed vs. economics and so on), he may formalise his intention and the mobility provider needs to provide a transaction processing facility.

At the end of the process, the mobility provider may have charged the customer a nominal fee for usage of this service. However, the underlying

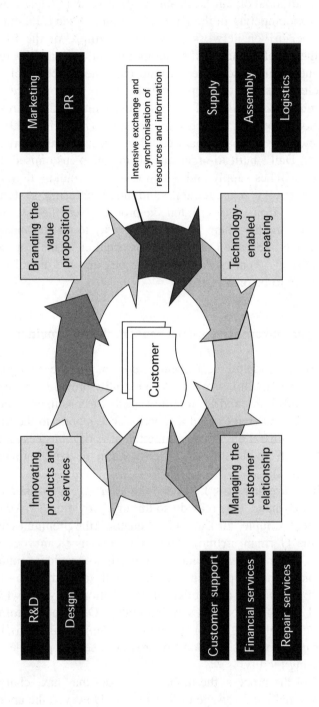

Figure 3.8   The customer-driven network for the automotive industry

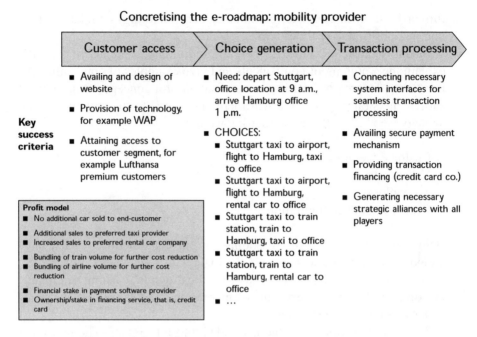

Figure 3.9   Value proposition of a mobility provider

traditional car manufacturer has not sold a single additional car, although he is about to make money. One possible profit model could entail generating revenues from selling cars to the taxi operators, additional car sales to the rental agency, further bundling travel volume with the airline for further price reductions, taking financial stakes in the transaction processing facility, and so on.

Figure 3.9 shows how a traditional car manufacturer may rather easily become a mobility provider, without cannibalising existing sales channels but by taking an active role in generating new market demand, effectively becoming a mobility facilitator.

After introducing our e-roadmapping tool and detailing two case examples, the next section will further concretise the e-roadmapping tool through our e-roadmapping index (eRI).

THE E-ROADMAPPING INDEX (eRI)

The eRI was constructed to concretise the strategy web concept and to facilitate measures of position (past and future) and performance. The eRI can be used regardless of geography, industry, and life cycle stage. It can further be used in absolute (community benchmarking) or relative (firm internal: position over time) terms.

In this section, we will describe the individual elements of the eRI, explain the weighing of components and give examples of application. As mentioned before, the eRI is a concretisation of a concept we introduced earlier: the strategy web. We will therefore adhere to the structure of the strategy web and will use the four known axes:

- Customer centricity
- Value metrics
- Technology
- Organisational configuration.

Below, we will explain the reasoning for our construction of each individual dimension and will support our logic with some selected examples.

Our *customer centricity* axis has four focal points: customer intimacy, customer value, the degree of segmentation (and therefore customer understanding), and branding.

The *customer intimacy* topic is divided into four issues. The first issue measures a company's current position in the value chain and the subsequent distance of the company from the customer. The further away a company is from its customers, the less a company might know about the customer. The second issue measures the degree of integration a company achieves in utilising customer impulses. For example, are new product/service cycles initiated by customer feedback, is feedback merely considered, or do at best notorious complainers receive attention? Within this measure of integration, we further differentiate between active impulses, that is, customer feedback like complaints or laudatory messages, and passive impulses, like recorded customer behaviour or known patterns of preference. The third and fourth issues consider the extent to which customer knowledge is obtained and, further, what use is made of this information. For example, are customer databases and/or customer relationship management tools in use, what sort of analysis is carried out with these data, and so on?

The *customer value* sub-dimension of our customer topic considers the customer retention tools. Here we differentiate between the quality of products and services offered over the lifetime cycle of the customer, the susceptibility of the service offerings for repeat purchases, and the ability of the company to leverage the customer lifetime value concept. For example, has the company understood that the needs of the customer diverge over the lifetime cycle? If so, are the products and services sufficiently positioned to satisfy these needs? And lastly, are efforts made to offer services throughout the whole lifetime cycle, even in cases where no (own) products or services are available?

Taking care of the customer was, is and will be the central ability of organisations. Our high regard for a company's susceptibility to customer needs is reflected in our high rating of these first two topics.

While incorporated as the topic with the least weight, we included *degrees of segmentation* to assess how sophisticated the company in question is in its approach and understanding of the customer. Therefore, the three sub-issues chosen are meant to measure the company's ability to reach a distinct closeness to the customer. And while the three elements can be understood as stepping stones or levels of evolution, particularities of certain industries are taken into account in this measurement.

The *branding* issue is the more external dimension of customer centricity. Brand captures things like perceived value to the customer, which often plays out in non-material ways. For example, the Mercedes brand is probably the greatest asset for the company; and while it requires constant nurturing, the basic value is apparently present to the customer. And although it is hard to spell out the exact brand value, many customers are willing to pay a premium for owning and driving a Mercedes.

Branding is further separated into brand value and press coverage. With the item brand value we want to measure the impact and recognition of the brand in itself (absolute value) and in addition, take account of changes over time (change of value over time). Both measurements are highly subjective, yet brand recognition studies do exist and these can be (and are) used to define corridors of absolute brand value.

Press coverage as a smaller indicator just takes into account the prevalence of the brand name either through active reporting or through advertising, in all forms of publications. And while a general correlation between brand value and press coverage is assumed to exist, the relationship is not a linear and monocausal one, otherwise brand building could be merely reduced to a function of advertisement spending. As we presume this not to be the case, the differentiation of issues (brand value vs. press coverage) should be an important one for start-ups to study in order to obtain better brand value recognition (Table 3.1).

Our second axis, *value metrics,* is segmented into measurements of four topics, focusing on the cost to acquire and retain customers, the internal financial ratios, the external view through various lenses of market valuation, and lastly the ability to take advantage of time.

Table 3.1   The customer centricity axis

Dimension/Axis	Topic	Issue	Issue Components
Customer centricity	Customer intimacy	Proximity to customer in value chain	
		Integration of customer impulses	Active, that is, complaints
			Passive, that is, customer behaviour
		Degree of customer knowledge	
		Use of data mining tools	
	Customer value	Life cycle products and services	
		Repeat offering susceptbility	
		Leveraging customer lifetime value	
	Degree of segmentation	Mass marketing	
		Focused segmentation	
		1:1 marketing	
	Brand	Brand value	Absolute value
			Change of value over time
		Press coverage	General newspapers
			Industry publications
			Online presence
			TV presence

In judging a company's ability to create measurable value, our first look is at the *customer cost* topic. Questions like how much investment is necessary to acquire a customer (in absolute and relative terms) need to be answered. Once a customer is acquired, the next question pertains to the company's cost and ability to retain the customer.

Our second topic, the internal performance or financial *ratios*, takes a closer look at operational metrics, their systemic use, and their overall quality as a governance tool. Governance metrics as an issue is exemplified here with sub-issues from an online venture. These operational performance metrics will differ naturally by type of industry and business. In the case of our online firm, operational performance is measured by the cost of generating interest, and cost of attaining an order. Overarching measures like the number of visits, number of page impressions and the conversion rate provide a good indication of a competitive positioning. At the end of the day, the combination of different technical, financial, and other governance metrics should enable the executive board to manoeuvre the firm through their daily operations. The second issue of the internal ratio topic is the measurement of the systemic use of metrics. The real question here is whether or not a system of metrics has been established to incorporate on the one hand supplier, partner, and customer metrics, and, on the other hand, to measure the management of the internal knowledge. Once the level of use is determined, a second look is taken at the four individual levels and their systemic use of metrics. The third issue of the ratio topic concerns the overall quality of metrics in use. That is to ask whether or not this company has a good system of metrics in place and whether or not these metrics then are any good to lead this company operationally day by day. This very last issue will clearly unveil how much brain work has been put into the conception of the daily operations of the firm.

Next to the internal valuations, the third topic is concerned with the *market valuations* of the company. The measures employed here merely reflect the methods used in today's investment banking and venture capital scene. No judgement or preference on any particular measure is taken, as this topic is only meant to signify an excerpt of conventional valuation methods. And by all means, markets after all will usually loudly declare their opinion on the various business value propositions.

The last topic of our value metrics dimension deals with the topic of *time*. The essence of time and the value of timeliness for the success of businesses has been emphasised for a long time. But as economies and markets seem to subjectively increase even further in speed, we deemed it necessary to measure a company's performance on a number of time-critical issues. The detailed issues relate to the performance of a start-up company as well as to established corporations. Where specific measures did not seem to apply directly (that is, start-up vs. incumbent player), a transfer of comparable measurements was taken. Our time measures start with the inception of the venture and proceed along the life cycle all the way to the maturation of the firm. With this measure we are able to capture issue-specific performance as well as the continuity of the performance. This time measure provides a good overall indication of business progress and the sustainability of success (Table 3.2).

Our third strategy web dimension is *technology*. Technology here is viewed from a pure technology and an applied (front-end, back-end and ASP) point of view. As this book is concerned with companies of and in the Digital Economy, all firms will have to show their aptness in dealing with the medium Internet. Technological savvy is therefore a must as it might be used in the deployment of a sales channel, or dealings with suppliers and

Table 3.2   The value metrics axis

Dimension/Axis	Topic	Issue	Issue Components
Value metrics	Customer cost	Customer acquisition cost	
		Customer retention cost	
	Ratios	Governance metrics	Cost per interest
			Cost per order
			Number of visits
			Number of page views/impressions
			Conversion rate
		Systemic use of metrics	Customers
			Internal knowledge management
			Suppliers
			Partner
		Quality of metrics (as a governance tool)	
	Market valuation	Earning multiples	
		Earnings per share	
		Future EPS	
		DCF	
		NPV	
	Time to development	Time to capital/funding	
		Time to market/launch	
		Time to brand	
		Time to scale/dominance	
		Time to IPO	
		Time to profitability	

marketplaces may require it. Or, a product or service offering may rely on a deep knowledge of such technology. And even those of us who still think technology is a toy for the nerds might want to contemplate Andy Grove's exclamation of the recent past, foretelling the demise of any and all companies not being or becoming digital in the very near future.

The first topic of the technology axis measures the know-how and application of *pure technology*. The issues we present here are meant to signify a path of technological evolution. And while these issues are only the tip of an iceberg, application of any of these technologies should suffice as indications of technological aptness. Take the simplified example of a consumer-market focused (B2C) start-up, which uses the Internet as the sole sales channel, utilising just HTML as their programming language. Our analysis here suggests that this company has missed the boat on technological advancements. Not even explanatory attempts to allow for old browser versions or slow Internet access connections can explain this delay.

Our second topic is concerned with the *front-end* technology. The issues at stake here are how well and to what extent customers are integrated in the front-end processes. Is, for example, technology used well to ease the customer into making repeat purchases, that is, does the customer need to re-enter critical information every time he/she enters, or is this information taken once and then stored securely for easy retrieval at the time of return? More important is the measurable ability to conduct the full transaction online and seamlessly. Points of measurement are the order entry and order management processes, the invoicing and payment processes, and the delivery and after-sales service processes. Every step that needs to be moved offline or cannot be conducted seamlessly, decreases the efficiency on the customer's as well as on the company's side.

Even more critical for success for most companies will be the performance on our third topic: the *back-end* technology. The issue here is not whether one managed to install a stand-alone enterprise resource planning (ERP) system such as SAP's R/3 or Oracle's Suite of Applications. Rather, the issue is one of seamless integration of all transaction data. For example, is information about planned production readily available to my suppliers, and does my change in forecasting initiate an automatic change in the order with the supplier, or is the supplier even involved in the forecasting of market needs? In addition to the IT-based integration of suppliers, questions pertain to the integration of logistics and other partners as well as to the communication ability between my financial planning software, my warehouse, and my customer databases. Lastly, one needs to show technological savvy on the fulfilment of standards. Measurements here are taken with regard to the scalability of applications, their compatibility, their security, and their portability.

Our fourth topic deals with *ASP*: application service provision. Being able to deal with application service provision is in our opinion a good indicator of how open the technological architecture of the company has been designed. It will show any forward looking planning with regard to implemented standards; a company in such a situation will easily be able to make use of ASP services and therefore outsource non-critical processes and applications.

One step further advanced is the company that can actually offer application services to others. This does not require all companies to actually become ASPs, but with this criterion we can evaluate with how much foresight the company has planned and implemented their applications, that is, are the processes state-of-the-art in the industry and could they therefore be

Table 3.3   The technology axis

Dimension / Axis	Topic	Issue	Issue Components
Technology	Pure technology	HTML	
		Java	
		XML	
		Other (eXML, OBI)	
	Front-end	Customer integration/linkage	
		Transaction processing (off- vs. online)	Order entry and management
			Invoicing
			Payment
			Delivery
			After-sales service
	Back-end	Supplier integration	
		Systems integration	
		Logistics integration	
		Other partner integration	
		Standards connectivity	Scalability
			Compatibility
			Security
			Portability
	ASP	Ability to use ASP services	
		Ability to offer ASP services	

made available to other companies, for which this application would bring great benefits? If this sort of question can be answered positively, it would be an indication of the company's superior technological position (Table 3.3).

Our last dimension is called *organisational configuration* and is simply a measure of the organisation's ability to cope with markets. Coping with markets naturally relates to capabilities of human resources. A company's ability to understand today's market and anticipate the needs of tomorrow's markets will remain one of the most critical factors on the survival and success path. The six *market reaction mechanisms* we identified and categorised are as follows: the first element judges the system in place for incorporating customer and supplier information, and in particular, the use of this information for forecasting and reaction purposes. The second issue merely evaluates the use of external information. That may be publicly available information, purchased reports or commissioned studies. The importance is with the concerted attempt for neutral views and opinions.

The third issue analyses the degree to which external information is then compiled and systematically used for acting and positioning in the market.

That is to say, if a trend change is assumed, what information and what further parties are included in the decision-making process for coping with this change? The fourth issue evaluates the internal efforts of the company to develop new products and services. What are the targets for development and how is this innovative ability facilitated and maintained? The fifth issue evaluates the sales channels used by the company and their respective mix. The sixth and last issue deals with the question of how new and/or old intermediaries are integrated in the organisation.

The second organisational configuration issue is the *people* issue. How are you maintaining a continuous scan and opinion on the market of the future, and who are the people carrying that knowledge? Are these individual functional experts? Are these product/service/segment specific executives? Who are other knowledge carriers? The importance in scoring on the people topic is a company's overall awareness of this critical topic through installing some sort of routine. Further evaluations pertain to the mix of experts and the ability to replace these key people in due time, that is, strategy for the war for talent and the overall structuring of compensation packages.

The third topic evaluates the *value creation* process. The first issue seeks to measure how well (and to what extent) the company has restructured value creation activity in response to the Digital Economy. Has the new environment been taken seriously? Have appropriate analyses led to changes in value creation processes, or is it just business as usual? The second issue measures the company's ability to act in co-opetitive mode. That is to say, has the company been able to partner with complementary organisations and how are they managing this partner network of greater complexity? The last issue of value creation assesses a company's progress on digitising the value creation processes. Progress can be measured in terms of digitised supportive processes, such as utilisation of electronic procurement applications, up to the company's ability to transform their products and services into digital value propositions.

The fourth topic rates the *revenue model* of the company. The first issue here is a relative evaluation of the innovation of the used revenue model. The answer to this key question should spell out the competitive lead the organisation has been able to generate. The second issue is concerned with the sustainability of the revenue model and its scalability. Questions regarding the commoditisation of services or potential loss of unique selling propositions need to be answered. If the revenue model is found to be sustainable, then the potential for worldwide scaling needs to be answered, as the second part of this issue will be a good indicator of growth and profitability perspectives. The third issue will evaluate the mix and diversity of revenue drivers. In our view, it is important to build a

Table 3.4   The organisational configuration axis

Dimension/Axis	Topic	Issue	Issue Components
Organisational configuration	Market reaction mechanisms	Systematic use of customer and supplier information	
		Market research	
		Integration of supplier and customers in solution development process	
		Company product and service development and research	
		Distribution channel portfolio	
		Intermediary integration	
	People	Key decision makers	
		Functional/technological experts	
		Process-aligned knowledge carriers	
		War for talent strategy	
		Compensation package	
	Value creation	New economy alignment of value creation elements	
		Organisation of partner network	
		Digitalisation of value creation	
	Revenue model	Innovativeness of the revenue model, and the implicit competitive lead	
		Sustainability and scalability of the revenue model	
		Portfolio mix of revenue drivers	

revenue model on a foundation that incorporates hedging risks through applying the portfolio concept (Table 3.4).

While it is our intention to lay open all elements used in calculating the eRI, the particular mathematical model, including the specific weighing, is omitted for reasons of maintaining intellectual property rights.

Offer to readers. Anyone interested in finding out the specific eRI value of his/her company, especially in contrast to other companies, may do so by submitting a request to the authors via the book homepage *www.e-roadmapping.org*.

We have used the above-mentioned particular content constellation for computing the specific eRI values of our showcases. The computations we performed allow an absolute comparison of the strategy and competencies of all companies involved. As we further analysed each case and articulated additional recommendations for each company, the future eRI value is also depicted and contrasted with the status quo.

Figure 3.10 gives a graphical depiction of the e-roadmapping index (eRI).

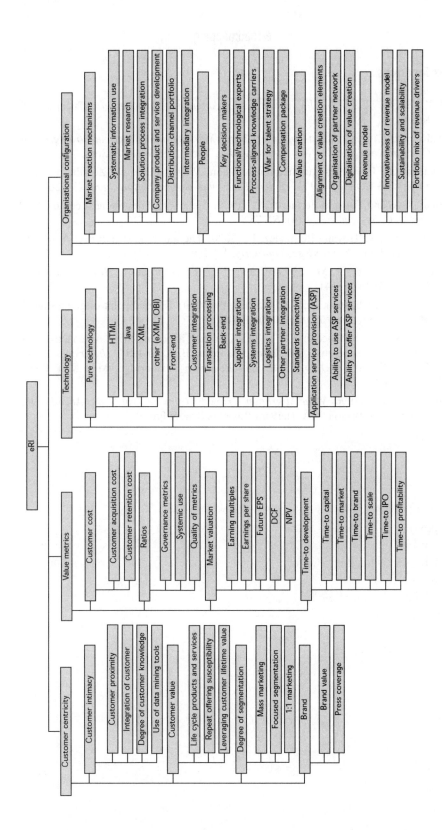

Figure 3.10 The e-roadmapping index (eRI)

References

A.T. Kearney (1999) *E-tailing Strategies for Automakers and Dealers*. Chicago: A.T. Kearney.

Aldrich, D.F. (1999) *Mastering the Digital Marketplace: Practical Strategies for Competitiveness in the New Economy*. New York: John Wiley & Sons.

Dudenhöfer, F. (1999) Automarken auf dem Weg ins Internet-Zeitalter: Einige empirische Befunde. *Jahrbuch der Absatz- und Verbrauchsforschung*, (3): 264–83.

Ealey, L.A. and Troyano-Bermúdez, L. (1996) Are automobiles the next commodity? *The McKinsey Quarterly*, (4): 62–75.

Ealey, L.A. and Troyano-Bermúdez, L. (2000) The automotive industry: A 30,000-mile checkup. *The McKinsey Quarterly*, 1: 72–9.

Hagel, J. and Singer, M. (1999) Unbundling the corporation. *Harvard Business Review*, **77**(2): 133–41.

Marshall, J.F., Christner, R.S. and Almasy, E. (1999) The real point of going digital. *Mercer Management Journal*, (11): 37–48.

Orlikowski, W.J. and Iacono, C.S. (2000) The truth is not out there: An enacted view of the 'digital economy'. In E. Brynjolfsson and B. Kahin (eds), *Understanding the Digital Economy: Data, Tools, and Research*. Cambridge, MA: MIT Press, pp. 352–80.

Slywotzky, A.J. (1996) *Value Migration – How to Think Several Moves Ahead of the Competition*. Boston, MA: Harvard Business School Press.

Introduction to the Cases

Chapter 4 aims to show some e-business in action in connection with our e-roadmapping tool. We chose the cases from the widest possible variety of dimensions. First, we have contributions from two Old Economy (Siemens and Daimler) and two New Economy (GoIndustry and getmobile.de) firms. We also have two business-to-business (B2B) and two value chain cross-over cases (Siemens, GoIndustry, and Daimler, getmobile.de).

Readers should be able to find a segment of interest to them as depicted in Figure 4.1.1.

This chapter will begin with a bridging note contributed by Johannes Schmohl from marchFIRST; the purpose of this note is to detail the evolution of business models and provide some insights from many implementation projects on the pitfalls and challenges of e-business projects.

This experience report should give the reader a fast entry on the learning curve for the design, conception and realisation of e-business projects.

The actual case part consists of individual case contributions from the above detailed companies. These contributions were written up for the sole purpose of this e-roadmapping book. They are not intended to show the

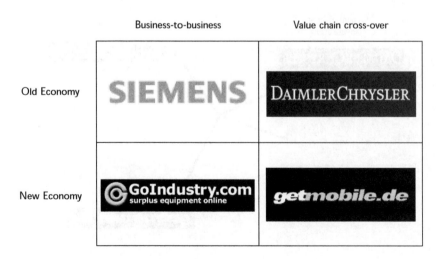

Figure 4.1.1   Case matrix

effectiveness of the e-roadmapping tool, but to give the full context of a whole e-business project, which we could not have provided through desk research, mere interviews or an external case study write-up.

The connection to our e-roadmapping tool will be provided in a two-fold manner. First, each particular case study was chosen because of its proximity to one of the four e-roadmapping strategy web dimensions (cf. Figure 4.1.2). This particular emphasis on one dimension of the strategy web for each case is used to show particular bits of innovativeness or state-of-the-art development within the e-business case in question.

The second tie-in with our e-roadmapping tool is that at the end of each individual case an e-roadmapping analysis with recommendations for future developments is provided for. This e-roadmapping analysis; and subsequent scoring of the eRI; was done in the most objective manner, yet was deemed fair and correct by the companies involved.

Therefore, this chapter provides the reader with cases focused on every single axis of the strategy web and at the end provides a thorough analysis of each e-business project through the application of our eRI. The reader receives up-to-date real-life case examples, with all the required context and content, and in addition receives a true application of the e-roadmapping tool. In the end, this should enable the reader to receive insights from the actual cases and the e-roadmapping analysis.

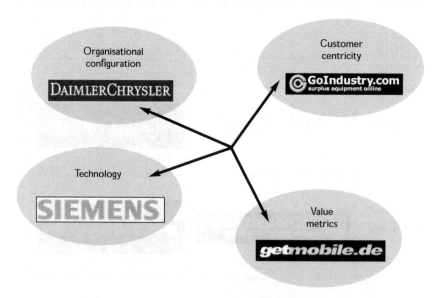

Figure 4.1.2   The strategy web and the cases

Materialising e-business: From Idea to Realisation

Johannes Schmohl, Senior Manager, marchFIRST

Preface

The identification and successful implementation of e-business strategies is neither a complete mystery nor a simplistic mechanism of putting business ideas on the Internet. Successful e-businesses will be the result of a profound strategy development and the 'zero-error' execution in an often difficult to define and rapidly changing environment.

On the strategic level an 'attacker' mindset is essential. It is critical to focus on sustainable value creation and aggressive growth in developing an e-business strategy, rather than focusing exclusively on 'defensive' moves and/or productivity/efficiency gains. As is often the case in traditional (non-Internet) corporate initiatives, the most ambitious online strategies have higher complexity, risk and cost but also higher ultimate reward if successfully implemented.

Three 'generic' paths exist:

1. Add value to an existing business or distribution channel by improving its efficiency
2. Create a new distribution channel where one does not currently exist
3. Create an entirely new business proposition leveraging e-technologies.

Only the last approach will offer the opportunity to proactively create significant value and not exclusively focus on the protection of an existing franchise. Although the majority of bricks-and-mortar based companies are most likely to start with the first strategy, they need to determine very early whether this is their ultimate business target or just an intermediate stage.

At the operational level, differences in performance do also have a direct impact on value creation. This is especially important as it is often in operations where the unfamiliarity with the online business logic of customer acquisition and retention as well as organisational and cultural implications lead to underperformance or failure.

This sub-chapter highlights the underlying logic and the pitfalls related to the identification of an e-business idea, its design and finally its implementation with all its operational implications (for overall concept see also Figure 4.2.4).

As the initial development of customer-focused e-commerce ventures both in the B2B and B2C space is maturing it will be more and more difficult to enter a customer-oriented business from a start-up position. Leading bricks-and-mortar players will be in the best possible position to leverage existing assets and translate them into an unsurpassable competitive advantage.

Therefore the following text is predominantly based on recent experiences of B2B and B2C clicks-and-mortar players entering into the e-business space. The examples worked into this text focus primarily on new business development but cover also many aspects of e-strategies driven by efficiency improvement and new channel creation. The reader will find at the same time many of the explications and examples applicable in a pure start-up environment.

In the recent past the author has worked closely with leading players in the retail, consumer goods and financial services industries as well as with venture holding and incubation organisations across Europe and North America. He is currently a Senior Manager in the Strategy Practice of marchFIRST, a leading global Internet professional services firm.

Idea identification

e-business ideas are countless and multiplying rapidly. They develop out of the desire to create value for both customers and shareholders through an e-business initiative. Most often ideas are based on reducing complexity or adding speed, convenience, information, and value for money in many aspects of corporate and personal life. Every organisation hopes to identify the next 'killer application'. But what looks like an ingenious process of developing breakthrough ideas has much more to do with the careful examination of an opportunity space, the assessment of existing assets to be leveraged and the identification of a market opportunity.

It is also evident that only part of the answer is contained in company-specific and market characteristics; but another key part of the answer lies within the company's risk appetite, sense of competitive urgency, and strategic ambitions. These latter factors need to be assessed as thoroughly as the former ones to determine the optimum e-business strategy for a particular company.

Opportunity space

Opportunity space is the set of possible options to introduce e-strategies in a corporate environment. Thereby an organisation is seeking to leverage the potential of new, networked and Internet-based technologies to create additional value by either improving the existing franchise or building new businesses.

In its most 'generic' definition, three different paths exist:

1. *Add value to an existing business or distribution channel by improving its efficiency*
   These are initiatives aiming to increase speed, lower cost and improve the efficiency of an existing franchise through competitive leverage and process improvement. The related applications have either an internal focus like knowledge management, sales force automation and training or an external focus when related to e-procurement, supply chain and distribution networks or recruiting. This alternative represents the lowest risk and is often an entry point for bricks-and-mortar organisations in approaching e-strategies.

2. *Create a new distribution channel where one does not currently exist*
   This set of strategies is aiming to create a new distribution channel in parallel to an existing bricks-and-mortar channel to compensate for the decline in existing channels and/or generate additional volumes. This will also allow the building of a predictive capability to anticipate where the market is headed next.

3. *Create an entirely new business proposition leveraging e-technologies*
   Just applying e-strategies to improve efficiency and create new sales channels will in many circumstances underleverage the potential to create value. The definition of entirely new value propositions focused on providing infrastructure, innovating and managing product/content

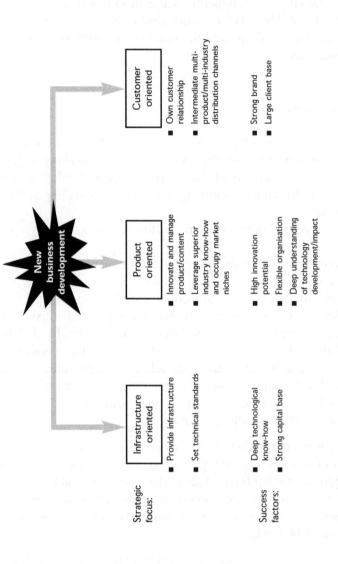

Figure 4.2.1 e-business orientations for new business development

or owning the client relationship is driving the development of new e-businesses (Figure 4.2.1). This strategy has the highest risk attached to it and can develop into a real internal competitor for the existing bricks-and-mortar business on the market as well as for internal resources. Some companies have even gone as far as to prioritise the new business development compared to the existing franchise by following a 'destroyyourbusiness.com' strategy.

To further discuss the business design and implementation phase of such newly created e-business is the key focus of this section.

Asset leverage

At the initial starting point for a new business the existing assets of the incumbent organisation – be it customer base, physical assets such as production and distribution facilities, company-specific know-how and the existing relationship network – need to be evaluated carefully. In many cases of mature bricks-and-mortar industries this might be a non-trivial undertaking, requiring a creative translation of existing assets into a clear competitive advantage.

Example 1 – How to leverage a bricks-and-mortar asset base

The following example of a leading incumbent player in the food distribution industry with a well established home delivery business, illustrates that an existing bricks-and-mortar asset base in a mature business can be translated into very attractive growth opportunities in an e-business environment:

- *Opportunity 1: exploit existing customer information*

Exploit the full value of customer information currently buried across multiple customer databases to boost existing business through a revised marketing approach. Such a program will rely upon micro-segmentation of the existing customer data to define highly focused direct marketing and communication campaigns targeting each customer's specific needs, desires, and spending patterns.

- *Opportunity 2: develop online customer interface*

Develop an online presence to market the existing products and services to a wider audience than the existing client base. Such a solution might be simply a communications channel or a more complex order placement front.

- *Opportunity 3: launch intermediation portal*

Launch an independent online brand targeting the existing customer base with a new and/or enlarged product and service offering, based on an intermediation business model. Prior experience in the US suggests that, for example, 'silver surfers' can provide

---

an attractive customer base – and the food distributors already own high penetration in this area.

- *Opportunity 4: leverage distribution infrastructure for e-business fulfilment services*

Leverage distribution infrastructure and provide 'e-fulfilment' services to third-party e-commerce firms, based on their specific skill sets. Home-delivery services operate a trusted delivery network across a wide region, have a large client base and profound marketing skills.

Access to customer base – A food distributor can offer contact with a 'home-delivery-familiar' customer base and association with a brand name, which customers already trust to deliver goods to their homes.

Delivery and logistics – A food distributor can exploit its existing logistical capabilities to fulfil orders placed online for additional goods and services. The level of logistical support required to deliver goods to customers is beyond the reach of many small companies (or delivery by larger companies is regarded as more reliable by consumers). This lack of (or perceived lack of) logistical support available to small companies may restrict customers to purchasing with known and trusted retailers. The e-fulfilment services, available at incremental cost to a home-delivery food distributor would surpass anything an e-commerce start-up could provide without outsourcing all its functions to a logistics provider. Furthermore, should our sample player prove successful in this area (and thereby generate liquidity) it may be able to bundle logistics needs from several e-commerce firms and thereby reduce the overall delivery cost.

Market opportunity

While the issue of asset leverage is solely based on internal competencies, an external view needs to be included as a starting point for an e-business initiative. Thorough industry comprehension combined with continuous and systematic market scanning activity will continuously generate opportunities. With the inherent knowledge of an industry the viability of these opportunities can be matched against market realities and a subsequent business proposal can be drafted. Thus this window on outside opportunities might have been institutionalised merely for purposes of competitive intelligence, but will now also serve as a systematic opportunity identification tool.

Example 2 – How to leverage market opportunities

The following example of a major retail industry illustrates how the overall emergence of e-business strategies is beginning to impact industry landscapes and therefore creates opportunities for first-movers, both leading incumbent players and start-ups which rapidly try to enter via market niches :

- *Opportunity 1: Industry redefinition*

During a phase of rapid convergence across many markets it becomes increasingly difficult to identify clear-cut industry definitions. Value bundles overlap heavily and the relevant set of competitors is changing quickly. Candidates driving a retail category portal could be, for example, retailers, consumer goods manufacturers, industry buying associations, existing portals and bargain sites. Intermediation and disintermediation strategies allow the creation of new business opportunities:

Intermediation – horizontally: Existing on- and offline players, not necessarily even directly linked to an individual industry, have begun to intermediate other businesses based on a strong brand and an appealing core value proposition (product comparison, price and so on).

Disintermediation – vertically: With the Internet facilitating direct access to end customers businesses representing different steps of the value chain can compete for each single end customer.

- *Opportunity 2: Value migration*

e-commerce will affect value generation and migration of profit margins along three dimensions:

Channels – Significant revenue shift towards online channels. In combination with a limited market growth this could imply declining revenue for bricks-and-mortar channels in the long run and an increasing pressure to reduce costs. At the same time this will force an improved leverage of existing infrastructure for the fulfilment of online commerce.

Profit models – Product commoditisation and price transparency will further increase pressure on margins. As a result value-added services such as product information and after-sales services will need to be leveraged to achieve a higher contribution. However, during the initial growth phase they are most often offered at extremely low margins as well, if not for free.

Value propositions – Through the arrival of players from other industries and an increasing pressure on margins entirely new value propositions, mostly in the service arena can be created. For major retail categories the intermediation of additional products and services, the second-hand market, sophisticated service offerings related to shopping engines, lifetime product packages (including warranties, replacement, removal, and so on) as well as comprehensive financial services can create additional growth potential.

Design

A parallel view of the long and short term is the best approach to e-business design. That is, developing a longer term (that is, three to six years out) view of what the industry could look like, how value will be created and what the desired positioning within the landscape would be. In parallel developing a more tactical, highly iterative near-term action plan focused on placing targeted 'bets' by 'testing and learning' with an iterative approach to positioning, value proposition, business model, financial modelling and corporate design – guided by the longer term view.

Positioning

Reflecting the three orientations while building an e-business – infrastructure, product or customer oriented – a multitude of specific positions can be occupied in the C2C, B2C and B2B space (Figure 4.2.2).

In the early stages of e-business development many clicks-and-mortar players focus on a customer-oriented positioning in order to leverage their existing customer base. More specifically the portal and vortal (vertical portal) concept has been fundamental in influencing the business design of many players.

This is following the hypothesis that in the future transactions will be more and more intermediated rather than directly routed from buyer to seller. An intermediary will provide a market platform and attract buyers through value-added services closely linked to the available product and service categories (price comparison, product review, and so on).

e-business gameboard
Key segments

Back-end ◀──────────────────────────────────▶ Front-end

Infrastructure oriented	Product and content oriented	Customer and supplier oriented	
■ Internet service provider (ISP) ■ Secure payment service provider ■ Application service provider (ASP) ■ …	■ Portal ■ Community	■ Auction sites ■ Classifieds ■ …	C2C
	■ Product information ('brochureware') ■ Product innovation, expertise	**Intermediation** ■ Portal ■ Hub ■ B2C verticals/horizontals **Direct supplier relationship** ■ Online shop	B2C
	External ■ Industry community ■ Online conferences **Internal** ■ Supply chain management ■ Knowledge management	**Intermediation** ■ Verticals ■ Horizontals ■ Trading hub **Direct supplier relationship** ■ e-procurement ■ Online shop	B2B

Figure 4.2.2   e-business positioning options

Increasingly, customers are going to conduct transactions online on an integrated platform. This integrated platform, the portal or marketplace, will include a wide variety of completely linked products and services, many of which will be intermediated and not 'manufactured' by the portal. Key components of the value propositions are process and price improvements as well as reporting and fulfilment services for B2B portals and information, communication, financial services and online shopping for B2C portals.

Based on its multiple revenue opportunities and the ability to lock-in customers over time, the attractiveness of the portal business case has already created intense competition among current players to establish leadership. In each industry and geographical market, only a limited number of players will successfully establish major portals that create very significant shareholder value. In this perspective, established players have a significant advantage due to their large customer base and strong brand. However, they will be faced with an intense rivalry between key players from different starting positions. In the B2C space this will primarily be consumer retail organisations and publishing companies, financial services institutions, new portal players (for example Yahoo, MSN) and e-retailers from specific retail categories (for example Amazon).

In addition to general portals, category-specific vortals (portals with a strong vertical focus, either by industry (B2B) or by interest (B2C)) are emerging, covering all needs of potential customers within a certain domain related to a distinct subset of their needs (for example travel, financial services, information, special interests such as sport, music or home, food …). Internet pureplays and a rapidly increasing number of traditional players have started to build such vortals for many industries but as yet dominant players seem to have evolved only in very few markets.

Value proposition

Within a portal or marketplace positioning, a winning value proposition needs to be precisely defined. At the moment e-commerce is perceived as one of the most important retail channels of the future. However, from a customer perspective, the combination of on- and offline value propositions within a clicks-and-mortar business model could become a very advantageous design. This seems applicable especially for retail industries with service-intense and sometimes difficult to explain products (Figure 4.2.3).

Each component of the value proposition needs to be defined and evaluated along certain criteria. The value proposition will also need to reflect

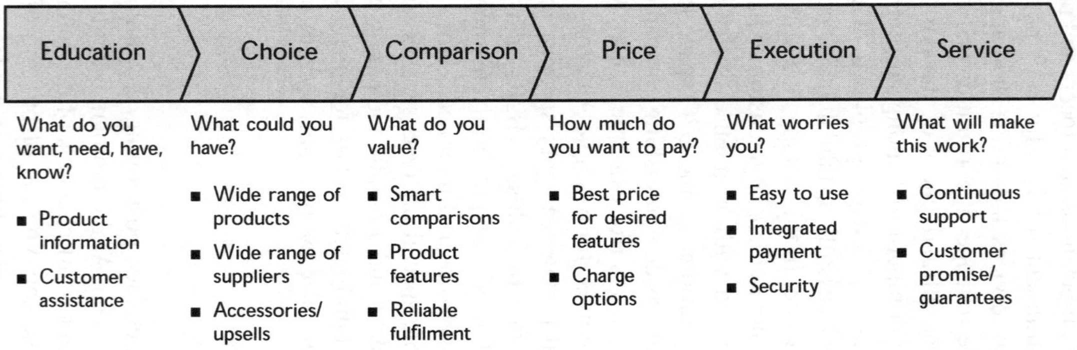

Education	Choice	Comparison	Price	Execution	Service
What do you want, need, have, know?	What could you have?	What do you value?	How much do you want to pay?	What worries you?	What will make this work?
▪ Product information ▪ Customer assistance	▪ Wide range of products ▪ Wide range of suppliers ▪ Accessories/ upsells	▪ Smart comparisons ▪ Product features ▪ Reliable fulfilment	▪ Best price for desired features ▪ Charge options	▪ Easy to use ▪ Integrated payment ▪ Security	▪ Continuous support ▪ Customer promise/ guarantees

Figure 4.2.3 Definition of value proposition – example portals and marketplaces

potential competitors and the target customer segments, which might be significantly different from the existing customer set in the case of a clicks-and-mortar environment.

- *Education* – precise information about the scope of the offering will allow the customer to develop interest and to verify an initial fit with his or her needs and expectations. Assessing these informational needs will allow definition of the depth and width of the required content of the online presence as well as the on- and offline communication strategy. The interactivity and educational aspects can be further enhanced by targeted (interactive) support functionalities.

- *Choice* – determining the optimum depth and width for an e-business value bundle becomes increasingly difficult. The focus on a large customer base and the ease of intermediation have led to increasing bundles of products and services being offered through one site or retail format. However, from a customer perspective there might be a limit to the scope of products and services that will be accepted from one single interface. This will mostly be based on the perceived expertise of a vendor and the basic trust of its brand and operations. The permanent change in scope and depth of the product and service offering of many players underlines the effort required to refine the fit with customer expectations. This implies a continuous search for the optimum breadth and depth of the product and service portfolio.

- *Comparison* – with the rapidly increasing choice and multitude of information which becomes available online, sophisticated tools to facilitate comparison and allow for increasing transparency of pricing and product features can become an important competitive advantage.

- *Price* – web-based technologies have helped to multiply pricing options for many products and services which had a fixed price defined by the seller before. Now buyer-driven as well as seller-driven pricing with fixed, variable (for example auctions) and 'free' (for example free ISP services) variants have emerged and can be applied to products and customer segments from which these models were previously excluded. Every e-business will need to define its most efficient price strategy and vehicle to communicate and sustain competitive pricing (for example price comparison tables, pan-European pricing …). However, at the same time the risks of cannibalisation of existing sales channels and 'content skimming' have to be evaluated.

■ *Execution and service* – in fully leveraging the capabilities of online commerce to create convenience and stickiness (mostly through responsiveness, speed, choice, transparency) it should not be forgotten that a very important part of any online value proposition will in many cases remain offline: fulfilment and after-sales services. Fulfilment will for most products and services remain a physical process, which needs to be linked closely into e-commerce and executed at a high level of service standards.

In addition the execution and service will need to respond proactively to customer concerns related to virtual business relationships, mostly responsiveness and security related.

The complexity related to execution and service continues to grow and thus favours players that have already demonstrated the ability to provide for such complex execution and have managed to create trust with their customer base.

Business model

The business model determines in which way an e-business is aiming to be remunerated and create value for its shareholders through a specific combination of revenue and cost models. Most important variables to define an individual business model are the revenue model, the variation between fixed and variable cost components and the extent to which value is being created inhouse or outsourced. The following explanations are entirely focused on pure online business models, which then can be blended with their offline counterparts in a clicks-and-mortar environment.

We can distinguish three generic models, which differ fundamentally in the way value is being created: facilitation, sales and intermediation business models:

■ *Facilitation* – e-businesses, which provide outsourced solutions for important business or customer-relevant functions (for example ASPs), tend to work with a large block of fixed costs related to the provision of complex functional and technology infrastructure. They will try to maximise the extent of stable revenues (for example fixed annual or monthly fees) to ensure coverage of the fixed costs. However, at the same time they will need to tackle the issue of increasing commoditisation of many products and services. Therefore, facilitation players will need to expand proactively from direct revenue sources (for example, selling their products and services online) to indirect ones (for example, advertising, data mining, and so on) and introduce on an ongoing basis innovative products and services.

- *Sales* – a traditional sales model based on a product margin will remain one of the most important business models. Costs related to manufacture of a product or service will often remain variable, but can be decreased substantially based on the economies of scale web-based technologies are offering in manufacturing or distributing these products or services.

- *Intermediation* – initially, portal players will earn revenue from both direct sources (for example, selling their products and services online) and indirect ones (for example, advertising, membership fees, sales of market reports or other third-party services, and so on). Subsequently however, the successful portals will also be able to leverage their customer relationship and intermediate products and services, which have been manufactured by a third party to expand their business proactively. The primary source of revenues will then become commissions on intermediated transactions – the T-tax (transaction tax). In this context players will try to minimise the number of variable cost components (for example no direct product cost in an intermediation model) and try to define most of the operating cost as fixed costs (for example outsourced technology or functional partners for the online presence). This can allow the creation of a highly scalable business model with an increasing return on any additional revenue.

The above business models are closely linked to the three orientations of building an e-business – infrastructure, product or customer orientation – described above. While infrastructure businesses will primarily adapt variants of facilitation business models, product businesses will focus on sales, and customer-oriented businesses on intermediation business models.

Financial modelling

When it comes to financial modelling the challenge is twofold: e-businesses will need to demonstrate a viable approach to achieve operational profitability quickly and at the same time ensure access to capital along the growth process of the company. Only under these conditions can the value for shareholders be continuously increased and a significant initial investment be justified.

Take-off and sustainability of the business will depend on the management of overall profitability, from high initial investment and negative returns, to break-even and positive returns supported by a strong growth in revenues (the J-curve).

High initial investments are driven by customer acquisition cost – even for incumbent players with a large customer base – and technology investments. Companies will tend to limit up-front investments but still need significant budgets for communication, product/technology development and infrastructure even if applying a phased approach to the most important items. In reality, substantial capital investments are still required, leading to break-off periods within the range of several years.

The challenge lies in the ability to identify attractive although realistic revenue streams in the beginning, and build a business case for a continuous medium- and long-term growth perspective that justifies the injection of additional capital along the way.

This is even more difficult as during the early stages of an online market segment total volumes tend to be very limited and even while growing at a rapid pace, significant volumes can only be achieved over time and by a very limited number of players in each market.

Relative to their longer-term development many players tend to justify revenue estimates based on their future leading position in an industry. However, it remains difficult to imagine that there will be more than a very limited number of players which will dominate a single segment (for example B2B vertical markets or B2C retail segments).

The hype of the early Internet years when relatively limited investment was sufficient to build a business and justify an Initial Public Offering (IPO) after several months at highly attractive payoff ratios has passed. Today's e-business projects are back to being evaluated in a more traditional capital budgeting manner, paired with some new metrics for evaluating strategic options.

The balance between short-term loss and medium-/long-term profitability remains a major challenge in financial modelling. Incorporating a 'real-options' approach to value the future potential also during the funding and investments process will facilitate the planning process.

Corporate design

Once the business and financial models have been defined, the design of an e-initiative does also include its corporate structure. Within a bricks-and-mortar context the question is therefore whether to develop a new e-business as a dot-corp unit within the existing corporate, as a completely separate dot-com entity or even as part of an entire venture portfolio. In this case the corporate would play the role of a business developer and investor for several e-business opportunities generated within or beyond its own organisation.

The decision to spin off an entity allows corporates to distribute risk, clearly isolate the negative cash impact and realise potential value within a shorter time frame. Many successful clicks-and-mortar entities, initially founded as spin-offs of large corporates, have demonstrated that significant value can be unlocked and a long-term growth strategy can be financed by the capital markets.

However, a detailed evaluation along strategic, financial and organisational dimensions seems to be necessary before a spin-off decision can be made.

From a strategic perspective it remains key that in any scenario the assets of the existing corporate are directly accessible to the new e-business and can be translated into a distinct competitive advantage. This must include access to the customer base, technological know-how or the cost-efficient sharing of support functions. But is the potential for synergies significant enough to justify a dot-corp design? The answer to this question will hinge mostly on the strategic intent of such an initiative. The closer the initiative is situated to the core competencies of the corporate the closer the alignment will need to be. However, even in non-dot-corp set-ups contractual agreements between the corporate and a separate e-business could possibly bridge separate entities and allow them to leverage areas of synergy, such as shared logistics.

Another strategic issue for consideration is the question of 'future options'. Does a corporation who decided to spin off an e-business initiative lose a valuable option on the future by doing so? Taking a 'real options' view, the spin-off could imply a limitation of the corporation to the role of cash-cow today with little growth potential for the future.

Leading players in the most innovative industries have even identified the need to enlarge their e-portfolios through new business development and intensify their own investment activity by launching venture capital and incubation arms. While such a portfolio will require significant investment budgets and very specific management skill sets it can provide an option to promote innovation, occupy market niches, generate long-term revenue growth and potentially obtain equity for service deals with some of the more cash-conscious e-businesses.

In addition to strategic concerns with dot-com entities, corporate investors tend to be wary about the financial perspective, linked to the cash impact of e-business initiatives and their implications on the corporate cash flow and overall company valuation. Shareholders of an incumbent player may prefer not to fund three to five years of expected losses, and therefore implementation may require a separate entity.

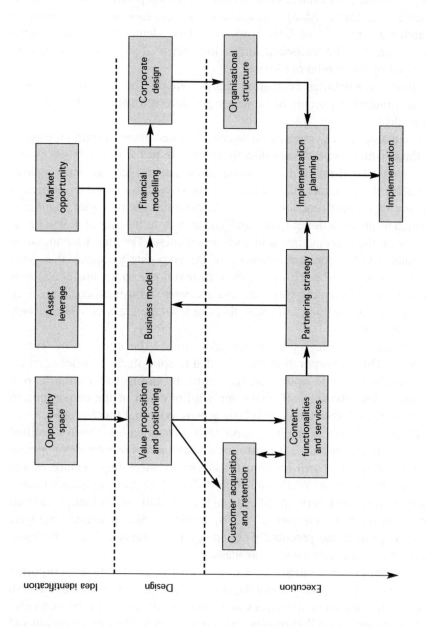

Figure 4.2.4 Materialising e-business – overall concept

While in the past capital markets rewarded corporates for spinning off their e-business initiatives in separate entities, the window of opportunity for such manoeuvres is heavily dependent on the fluctuations of market valuations.

Such moves tended to generate attractive returns for the investor at an IPO stage. The shareholders of the corporate in this case can benefit from the IPO proceeds most of the time. From a longer term perspective, however, shareholders might feel excluded from any later gains and the post-IPO capital appreciation, still based on the initial financing of the corporate and its shareholders.

From an organisational perspective, one area of concern has been the compatibility of organisational cultures between the existing corporate and the newly established e-business. Skill sets and motivation schemes which are very different from corporate standards may be required (see also 'Organisational and cultural implications' below). This divergence in requirements may well offset the synergy potential and warrant a more autonomous, that is, dot-com, design.

Taking into account these strategic, financial and organisational elements will allow a sensible decision on the corporate design for any e-business project.

Execution

After the idea identification and design phase, a rigorous execution completes the process of materialising an e-business (Figure 4.2.4). In the execution phase the most critical elements are the detailing of the value proposition, a successful customer acquisition and retention process, the thorough understanding of organisational and cultural implications as well as partnership development.

A first step requires a breakdown of the value proposition into a system of sub-value propositions. Within each of these, the unique selling points (USPs) are delineated. And based on these USPs the key content features and actual functionalities need to be defined to facilitate operational implementation. This means defining key features and describing each functionality at a very detailed level. Only through application of this top-down approach paired with rigorous project management can a successful implementation be achieved.

Figure 4.2.5 provides an example of how to compile a detailed list of content and functional components.

Sub-value proposition	Unique selling points	Key content features and functionality
'Your definitive source of information and educational resources'	▪ The widest educational resource ▪ Unrivalled multimedia resource ▪ Content specifically tailored to the needs of the teacher and pupil	**Functionality** ▪ Search engine to search for resource by subject, age suitability, topic, author, and so on ▪ File download system ▪ Webcasting system ▪ Content translation for foreign users **Downloadable content** ▪ Information packs on exhibits for teachers ▪ Worksheets for children's use ▪ Key resource packs on history, geography, politics and economics **Video and audio content** ▪ Library of video and audio content that can be watched online ▪ Dynamic presentations **Interactive content** ▪ Educational quizzes **Community** ▪ Chat forums for teachers, parents and children to discuss education issues **News** ▪ The latest news **Links** ▪ Links to other sources of useful information

Figure 4.2.5   Detailing of value proposition –
example information and education

Online business logic

The market is providing disproportionate returns to first movers. This reflects the importance of becoming one of the very few recognised leaders in a category and managing to build up quickly a large base of customers.

It is therefore, vital to practise an online business logic that reflects the following customer acquisition and retention mechanism (see also Figure 4.2.6):

1. *Attract visitors to the site*

   Most important here is the need for a systemic media mix for attracting visitors. Within the media mix the three categories of online communication, offline communication, and partnership need to be carefully balanced. Online communication relates to everything from banners to e-mails and newsletters. Offline communication covers selected magazines, and other more traditional media. And partnership details link exchanges, sponsoring and other co-operative efforts. Incumbent players can often benefit from a large customer base and a well-known brand.

2. *Transform visitors into prospects, and subsequently into clients*
   To transform visitors into clients an appropriate value proposition for the target client segment remains absolutely essential. Sophisticated presentation can enhance the actual offering, ranging from navigational tools to animated content and comprehensive value-added services.

3. *Generate loyalty with visitors and clients*
   Acquired customers need to be kept loyal through a personalised approach. Content offerings can be specified according to detailed profiles and dynamic profiling allows even the smallest segments ('up to a segment of one') to be addressed. The approach is complemented with continuously updated and relevant content.

4. *Continually attempt to differentiate your product and service offering from that of your competitors*
   Strategically, efforts need to be made continually to innovate and improve your product and service offering by maintaining the up-to-date status and a view on leap-frog developments.

Keeping an eye on the future (point 4) will help to achieve a position of competitive leadership and subsequently generate the target revenue levels.

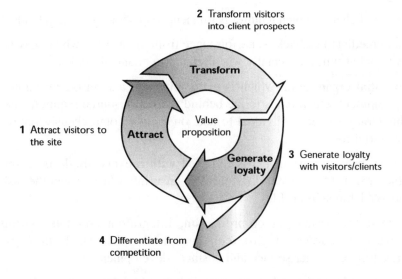

Figure 4.2.6   Online business logic

Organisational and cultural implications

Although incumbent players can have a strong starting base, due to their superior industry know-how, network and asset base, success is not assured. Specifically, winning will require a management approach that is highly counter-intuitive for many traditional organisations on both a corporate and an individual level.

On a corporate level decisions will be taking place in a much more uncertain environment than in the past, characterised by rapid changes in the market development and less precise planning data. The winners will have developed faster decision-making processes and will have learned to make decisions and place 'targeted bets' even without full information.

The depth of value creation within an organisation might be very limited, following a strong focus on either customers, products and services or infrastructure and fulfilment. For example in many cases successful portals will be supplying a product that is manufactured by a third party. Most traditional organisations, however, are more comfortable producing and selling their own proprietary products.

On an individual level the management needs to apply a new approach in order to ensure the motivation and performance of their organisation. The management style needs to reflect the following:

- An environment with a high degree of uncertainty concerning the longer term direction and even existence of the organisation

- A pace of change which requires permanent adaptations of each individual

- An immediate feedback on performance from the market, which may be irrational at times, especially when related to financial markets

- An initial organisation which is extremely light and an organisational development which tends to lag behind the real resource requirements. This requires every individual to take on a more comprehensive/entre-preneurial role

- A very broad range of skills required within every single position, which can lead to severe difficulties in ensuring a fit between the task and available skill profile

- A need for permanent co-ordination, integration and job sharing between resources of different disciplines, that is, technology, marketing, customer service and business development

- A workload which tends to be very substantial, often over significant periods of time.

Partnership development

A 'go-it-alone' strategy will just not be feasible, cost-effective and smart for most players. Any robust e-strategy needs to involve and leverage a set of alliances/partnerships with other industry players and third-party vendors. This will allow locking-in a critical mass of customers, providing highly innovative and specialised products and services, promoting technology platforms and setting proprietary standards. Organisations that have chosen to focus entirely on either infrastructure operations, product and service generation or customer and supplier relationship management will depend on strong partnerships to complete and effectively market their offering.

Summary

This sub-chapter is positioned between the e-roadmapping tool and the forthcoming company e-business case studies. The intention of this section was to materialise the process of an e-business creation from the initial idea identification to implementation. Numerous decisions that have to be taken along the way have been discussed and the subsequent steps of implementation highlighted.

In the e-business idea identification section, the concept of an opportunity space with its three generic options was introduced. The asset leverage and market opportunity view detailed the possibilities of an internal and external analysis, concluding with the necessity of combining these two complementary approaches.

Having identified the idea, the next logical step – design – was detailed. The design phase in an e-business has to cover the strategic positioning, the value proposition and business model definition, financial modelling and corporate design.

The last paragraph discussed and highlighted the detailing of an online value proposition as well as customer acquisition and retention, organisational implications and partnership development for a newly developed e-business.

The e-roadmapping tool laid the conceptional foundations for becoming a true e-business; this section helped to materialise these concepts by breaking them down to an operational level based on hands-on experience in implementing successful e-strategies for leading players in the retail, consumer goods and financial services industries.

The following company case contributions will further underline the above discussion and highlight additional issues in their specific industries.

getmobile.de: Digital Strategising of a High-growth Internet Start-up

Oliver Ohlen, Manager e-Commerce, getmobile AG

CHAPTER CONTENTS

Introduction

In March 1999, getmobile.de was founded by a team of management consultants, IT specialists, and marketing experts to create a business-to-consumer e-commerce shop for mobile communication devices and service plans. The company received its first round of financing in June 1999 and launched its service on 15 July 1999. The second round of financing closed in March 2000. By the end of the year 2000, getmobile.de and its subsidiaries had a workforce of 60 people and achieved 50 million DM in revenues. The headquarters of this e-commerce start-up is located in Munich, Germany. Getmobile.de's mission encompasses two building blocks: being *the* expert of mobile communication in the business-to-consumer market and being *the* e-services partner of the mobile communication industry. In order to finance its ambitious growth, the firm plans to make an IPO in 2001.

This contribution aims to depict the development path of getmobile.de's business model, market scaling, and internal venturing. In the following, the evolution from the initial business-to-consumer value proposition to the extension to the business-to-business area and to the offline world will be displayed. Subsequently, an outsider's view on the past achievements and the future possibilities through the application of the e-roadmapping methodology will be provided.

Development path of the digital strategy

The initial value proposition: business-to-consumer e-commerce

The business model

The German market for mobile phones and service plans is characterised by high non-transparency: the consumer has the choice among more than 2000 configurations of service plans and more than 60 mobile phones. The process of searching and comparing all these different offers and of getting a complete overview of what fits the personal needs best has been time-consuming and cost-intensive. Thus, customers have a clear need for orientation and advice in this market in order to make informed buying decisions according to their individual usage patterns and preferences.

This customer need has been the starting point to develop the business-to-consumer value proposition: by offering a comprehensive tariff calculator getmobile.de empowers the customer with detailed information as well as real-time and cost-efficient comparison of products and service plans on an individual basis. Getmobile.de covers the full product range of mobile phones and service plans from the majority of hardware manufacturers and service providers in the German market. Subsequently, the offered product range has been extended to other mobile devices such as PDAs (personal digital assistants), digital cameras, MP3 players, and accessories of all kind. Ordering is conducted online or via a call centre. Figure 4.3.1 illustrates customers' needs which are addressed by getmobile.de's business-to-consumer value proposition.

One important source of competitive advantage in the coming e-commerce shake-out will be fulfilment (Peet, 2000). Speed, reliability, and cost-efficiency in logistics and delivery are key success factors for outpacing the competition. Online ordering of mobile phones and service plans had been complicated, error-prone, and time-consuming for the consumer due to media disconnects and delivery times of up to three weeks. In co-operation with first-tier partners, getmobile.de has been able to develop and implement best-practice fulfilment and distribution processes: the customer benefits from the unique one-step order system and the delivery within 48 hours. The consumer gets in contact with getmobile.de only once and receives his activated mobile phone 48 hours after the online order. Customers can track and trace the status of their orders via the Internet. As a means of consumer protection and fraud prevention the delivery service checks the identity of the respective customer at the point of delivery. Figure 4.3.2 illustrates the one-step order process of getmobile.de.

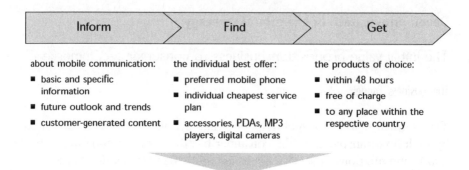

Inform	Find	Get
about mobile communication:	the individual best offer:	the products of choice:
■ basic and specific information	■ preferred mobile phone	■ within 48 hours
■ future outlook and trends	■ individual cheapest service plan	■ free of charge
■ customer-generated content	■ accessories, PDAs, MP3 players, digital cameras	■ to any place within the respective country

One-stop shopping for mobile communication

Figure 4.3.1   getmobile.de's one-stop shopping solution
for mobile communication devices

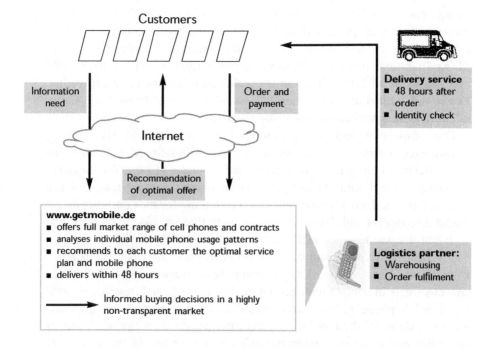

Figure 4.3.2   One-step order process

Partners

Since its incorporation, getmobile.de has built up an extensive network of partners in the offline and online world: mobile service plans are marketed from providers such as T-Mobil, D2 Vodafone, E-Plus, Viag Interkom, Cellway, Talkline, and so on. Cell phone hardware comes from leading manufacturers such as Nokia, Motorola, Siemens, Ericsson, and so on. Warehousing, fulfilment, and logistics have been outsourced to specialists. The final delivery to the customer is executed by DPD and OPC (logistics service companies). The parties involved are connected by a proprietary, Internet-based software that has been developed inhouse. The communication and information sharing between getmobile.de, service providers, credit investigation institutions, fulfilment, and delivery services in the order and fulfilment process are, to the greatest extent possible, automated and conducted online. In this complex process, getmobile.de acts as an anchor and orchestrates the extensive network of complementary partners and suppliers of outsourced functions.

In the Internet space, getmobile.de has been able to complement its product and service offering through strategic partnerships with leading Internet firms: for example, getmobile.de shops have been integrated into websites such as Yahoo Deutschland, Autoscout 24, and vivendo.de. Auctions of cell phones are provided by eBay. A tariff calculator comparing fixed-line telephony plans comes from specialist Teltarif.de.

Moreover, getmobile.de offers online shop hosting and maintenance, fulfilment and distribution to leading producers of mobile devices. The first solution has been implemented for Motorola, Germany. Other hardware manufacturers will capitalise on this service in the near future. Getmobile.de aims to become the partner of choice to perform electronic commerce for producers of mobile devices. Thus, additional demand and site traffic can be generated at virtually no marketing cost. Furthermore, revenues from software development and maintenance are being realised. Figure 4.3.3 shows the Motorola's online shop that has been realised by getmobile.de.

Market and competition

The mobile phone market in Germany grows dynamically: Plica market research predicts a CAGR (compounded annual growth rate) of 25 per cent in the 1998 to 2003 period. The number of users will increase from 13.8 million in 1998 to 41.1 million in 2003. Market saturation tendencies

get**mobile**.de

ONLINE KATALOG FUR

(M) *MOTOROLA* PRODUKTE

WEB WITHOUT WIRES

DIE GANZE WELT DER KOMMUNIKATION
IN EINER HAND

SO VERSCHIEDEN UNSERE
ANSPRÜCHE SIND, SO
VERSCHIEDEN IST AUCH
DAS ANGEBOT AN
MOTOROLA PRODUKTEN.
FINDEN SIE ONLINE IHR
PERSÖNLICHES MOBILTELEFON
VON MOTOROLA.

BESTELLUNG
ONLINE

| HANDYS | FUNKGERÄTE | ZUBEHÖR | PREPAID | TARIFE |

KUNDENDIENS

Deutschland ◆

Figure 4.3.3   Motorola's online shop realised and hosted by getmobile.de

after the year 2003 are expected to be compensated by technological progress in the area of broadband infrastructure (for example the global mobile communication standard UMTS) and in the area of hardware appliances (for example convergence of cell phones and PDAs). Despite these high growth rates, the competition in the German market is fierce: in 1999, more than 20,000 offline and online retailers competed for buyers of cell phones and service plans. In the offline world, competition encompasses the affiliated shops of the service providers, category killers, independent specialist stores, mail order businesses, and so on. In the online space, getmobile.de competes with the sites of service providers, mail order businesses, and specialised mobile communication shops. Getmobile.de differentiates itself from the competition by offering and comparing the full range of cell phones and service plans in the German market. No competitor currently offers the customer an equal level of information, transparency, and advice to identify and select the ideal combination of cell phone and service plan. Moreover, the one-step order and delivery process is a benchmark in the market.

The next phase – opening an additional channel with WAP

Although WAP (wireless application protocol)-enabled hardware and software are still in an infant stage as of today, the take-off of this technology is expected to happen in the near future: the next generation of mobile communication devices and the upcoming UMTS (universal mobile telecommunications system) standard will enable high-speed data transmission and a much wider range of multimedia services. By 2005, more people in the world will have mobile phones than TVs or PCs, which means that mobile communication devices could become the most important access device to the Internet (Kehoe, 2000).

Confronted with the above evidence, getmobile.de integrated WAP services in its value proposition. The primary goals of this effort were to step on the experience curve at an early stage of the technological evolution, to position its service in the major portals before the competition, and to open up a new sales channel. The initial business-to-consumer WAP offering encompasses transaction capabilities and information services. The customer has access to getmobile.de's shopping areas which are adapted to the specific requirements of mobile Internet access via WAP: as mobile Internet connections are still limited in transmission capacity and hardware devices need to be improved, ordering is conducted via a call-back functionality. After the consumer has made a choice, the call centre agent receives the order information and the customer's phone number by e-mail, calls the customer and finalises the order via phone. Thus, the mobile commerce value proposition opens an additional channel for getmobile.de to market mobile phones, service plans, accessories, and so on to the customer via WAP. Moreover, the customer has access to getmobile.de's information services covering the area of mobile communication. In the near future, it is planned to complement the WAP offering with unified messaging services as well as value-added content which will be provided by content partners.

Entering the business-to-business arena

The online marketplace tel2bmarket.net

The business model

The supply chain of mobile communication hardware and accessories in Germany is highly fragmented and non-transparent: it encompasses more than 20,000 players such as hardware manufacturers, net operators and service providers, brokers, distributors, offline and online retailers. As a consequence, the supply chain is characterised by inefficiencies such as the time-consuming comparison of offerings, a limited supplier and buyer universe, problems of availability and goods overhang. The subsidiary tel2bmarket.net AG has been founded to address and to reduce these inefficiencies. The core value proposition of this vertical, Internet-based marketplace is to organise and to facilitate the optimal allocation of supply and demand among the fragmented players in this market. The platform is tailored to the distinct needs of professional vendors and buyers in the mobile communication market: it integrates necessary market-specific elements such as distinct product specifications and a bargaining mechanism allowing participants to negotiate with several counterparts in real-time. Figure 4.3.4 displays the basic business model of tel2bmarket.net.

The basic idea of tel2bmarket.net is to create a spot market for mobile communication hardware and accessories. Participants can expand their supplier as well as their buyer universe at virtually no additional cost, allowing producers and intermediaries to offer excess inventory and to free liquidity by reduction of stocks. Intermediaries can post extraordinary demand and thus enhance the availability of products. Offers and requests of the participants are displayed anonymously by the system; the identity of the counterpart is revealed after a deal has been closed. Additionally,

tel2bmarket.net organises the optimal allocation of goods in the market

- No excess inventory/no depreciated goods
- Freed liquidity due to reduction of stocks
- Enhancing availability of products

Figure 4.3.4   The basic business model of tel2bmarket.net

tel2bmarket.net offers industry news, technical information, and hardware specifications as well as a discussion forum for the business community.

While transaction fees are tel2bmarket.net's initial revenue source, the service has tremendous opportunities to leverage additional sources of revenue: first, the company can capitalise on the masses of information which are gathered over time. As data are obtained and aggregated from the entire supply chain of the mobile communication market, the gathered information is expected to be of high validity and relevance. Thus, tel2bmarket.net will offer professional market intelligence services and will provide its participants with valuable information concerning industry trends, demand shifts, pricing, and so on. By versioning and pricing this information, the marketplace will aim at diversifying beyond transaction fees and will add an important value element to its customer service. Second, by offering online activation of service plans to retailers, tel2bmarket.net can generate revenues through commission fees that are charged for this service. The participating retailers profit from an increased independence of net operators and service providers and from a broader range of alternative service plans. Moreover, retailers can realise higher margins as tel2bmarket.net bundles demand and thus increases activation payments of service providers.

Partners

In order to obtain critical mass of participants and to ensure significant market liquidity, tel2bmarket.net has been able to leverage getmobile.de's existing contacts to manufacturers, net operators, service providers, and distributors. As a result, many core industry players had signalled their commitment to participate in this marketplace before launch. Three months after launch, tel2bmarket.net had over 600 registered corporate participants in the online marketplace leading to a traded volume of 4 million DM. These figures translate into a 5 per cent share of the targeted industry players. According to an investigation of Forrester Research (2000), corporate participants will look for electronic marketplaces to play dual roles in the near future: acting as a one-stop shop for a variety of products as well as offering highly specialised industry-specific services. Thus, tel2bmarket.net plans to integrate additional offerings such as credit and payment as well as distribution and logistics services. To accomplish this task, additional alliances with other marketplaces that cover these specific areas will be a necessary step.

Market and competition

According to Plica market research, the German business-to-business market of mobile communication hardware will increase from 13 million units in 2000 to 14.5 million units in the year 2002. This leads to a transaction value of roughly 5 billion DM in 2000 and 6 billion DM in 2002. Being the first mover in this market, tel2bmarket.net aims to rapidly achieve critical mass and to capture a share of this giant cake through transaction fees and other additional revenue sources. As mentioned above, tel2bmarket.net offers an unprecedented value proposition for players in the supply chain of mobile communication hardware: the service differentiates from alternative intermediaries by offering unlimited reach and a broad variety of offers and requests. Participants are enabled to expand their buyer and supplier universe at virtually no additional cost. Moreover, the platform intends to increase price transparency, to reduce excess inventory and problems of availability, and to lower transaction cost.

Becoming a virtual distributor – the acquisition of WAP Telecom

In October 2000, getmobile.de acquired WAP Telecom, a virtual distributor of mobile devices. WAP Telecom acts as a wholesaler of telecommunication hardware and accessories for the specialised retail sector and relies on the Internet as primary distribution channel. The firm aims to leverage the optimisation potential of online distribution such as actual information, rapid feedback to customer enquiries as well as cost reductions in order handling and fulfilment. WAP Telecom was founded by former leading executives of traditional distributors of mobile communication hardware. Thus, the firm combines a long-standing industry experience, in-depth market know-how, and established contacts to leading players with a flexible clicks-and-mortar business model. The backward integration leads to important advantages for getmobile.de: first, WAP Telecom contributes an important part to getmobile.de group's total revenues. Second, the purchase prices of mobile communication hardware and accessories are being reduced significantly. Third, the product availability is enhanced. Finally, WAP Telecom's extensive partner network and market knowledge can be leveraged for getmobile.de's different business models.

Mobile commerce with cardmaxx.de

With its subsidiary cardmaxx.de, getmobile.de and WAP Telecom have introduced a new and convenient way to reload prepaid vouchers via Internet, WAP or SMS. The cardmaxx.de technology enables consumers to easily reload their mobile phone prepaid vouchers at all times and independent from the actual location. The customer orders the desired amount of the new voucher via cell phone or Internet; this request is then transmitted from cardmaxx.de to the net operator or service provider which activates the customer's account and transmits the voucher identification number via cardmaxx.de to the consumer. Figure 4.3.5 visualises the basic functionality of the cardmaxx.de business model.

For its service cardmaxx.de charges the customer a small fee for each transaction. In addition to the basic revenue model of prepaid voucher reload, cardmaxx.de retrieves important customer data to make individual post-paid contract offerings and hence to transform prepaid clients into credit clients. Moreover, cardmaxx.de is a medium to distribute mass customised SMS.

Going offline through co-operation with Old Economy partners

On the basis of the assumption that the New Economy and the Old Economy will increasingly converge in the future, getmobile.de has established co-operation with Old Economy partners: for example, together with Tchibo, a German coffee shop that has extended its offering to rapidly

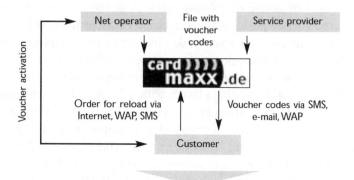

- Available to customers at all times independent from the actual location
- Substantial savings due to lean distribution process
- Information about customer behaviour patterns

Figure 4.3.5   Basic functionality of the cardmaxx.de business model

Figure 4.3.6   getmobile.de – partner of choice for Old Economy players

changing assortments of different consumer goods, getmobile.de has sold over 36,000 cell phones with prepaid vouchers in Tchibo's 940 German outlets. Or, together with McDonald's, Germany, getmobile.de has organised a sweepstake of 5000 cell phones. Getmobile.de's strategy is to strengthen the relationship to the offline world as distinct consumer segments are expected to demand a multi-channel purchasing experience that combines the Internet, call centre services, and physical stores. Hence, the firm aims to identify and to occupy promising market segments and business opportunities in the offline sector through partnerships with Old Economy players. Figure 4.3.6 displays the joint project of getmobile.de and McDonald's, Germany.

Summary – getmobile.de's digital strategy at a glance

In the previous sections, the development path of getmobile.de's business model from the initial business-to-consumer value proposition to the extension to the business-to-business area and to the offline world has been displayed. Table 4.3.1 summarises the business activities of getmobile.de and its subsidiaries. Additionally, it provides an overview of distinct strategic objectives, revenue models, and critical success factors (CSFs).

In the light of this contribution, one might hypothesise that, in the highly competitive telecommunication market and the rapidly evolving e-commerce environment, corporations have to constantly rethink their basic assumptions about customer relationships and business models in order to stay ahead of the competition. In this fast-changing, digital-enabled environment, firms need to keep asking themselves what business they are really in and which part of the value creation they will be able to perform better than current and potential rivals in the digital future. Moreover, as incumbents are beginning to flex their muscles in the online world, the success and sustainability of Internet start-up firms such as getmobile.de increasingly depend on superior speed of business model extension and market scaling, reliable fulfilment and logistic processes, and the formation of best-in-class partner networks.

The e-roadmapping analysis

Based on the case materials provided beforehand, numerous personal interviews and our continuous relationship with getmobile.de since its founding in

Table 4.3.1   getmobile.de's digital strategy at a glance

Business Model	Brand	Strategic Objectives	Revenue Model	CSFs
Business-to-Consumer	getmobile.de	■ Being the online market leader in Germany ■ Being the expert in mobile communication	■ Online sales ■ Sales via WAP channel ■ Shop hosting ■ Information brokerage	■ First-mover ■ Brand building ■ Fulfilment and logistics
Business-to-Business	tel2Bmarket.net	■ Being the leading online marketplace for mobile communications hardware	■ Transactions fees ■ Information brokerage ■ Commission fees	■ Critical mass ■ Software tailored to distinct industry needs
	WAP Telecom	■ Revenue enhancement ■ Reduction of purchasing prices ■ Enhanced product availability	■ Distribution of mobile devices	■ Industry experience ■ Market know-how ■ Relationships to market players
Mobile Commerce	cardmaxx.de	■ Reloading prepaid vouchers via mobile devices or Internet ■ Being first-mover and market leader	■ Transaction fees ■ Information brokerage ■ Mass customised SMS	■ First-mover ■ Partnerships with net operators and service providers
Offline Commerce	*co-operations*	■ Multi-channel purchasing experience ■ Leveraging offline business opportunities	■ Offline sales	■ Partnerships with offline players ■ Fulfilment

the spring of 1999, we were able to use our e-roadmapping index (eRI) extensively for scoring this company.

eRI score

Applying our eRI getmobile.de achieved the scores shown in Figure 4.3.7 in the areas of customer centricity, value metrics, technology and organisational configuration.

As we were able to apply a full e-roadmapping analysis to the getmobile.de case (see following section), our focus in the eRI analysis will lie exclusively on the value metrics dimension of our strategy web.

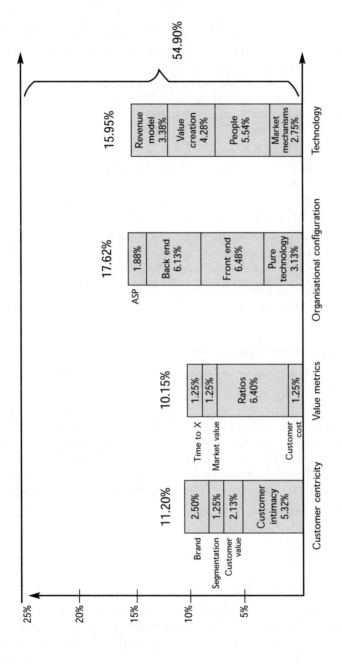

Figure 4.3.7 getmobile.de's eRI score

In the sub-dimension time-to-development, we first found a stringent belief in the necessity to manage by milestones. Second, the milestones time-to-funding and time-to-market/launch were achieved (a) within reasonable deviation from the initially set-out goal, and (b) by competitive measures in comparison to other German B2C retailers. The third measurement, time-to-brand is in active development. Clearly, branding efforts are a killer factor for such a broad retailer like getmobile.de, yet the brainless burning of cash for undirected marketing – as the many Boo's of this world have shown – is not the right recipe either. Concluding, the time-to-measurements are taken very seriously, with certain areas still being work in progress.

If we take a look at the ratios sub-dimension, we find a very strong showing in the area of online metrics. All the metrics we rated are being applied and are used for monitoring systemic progress. In conclusion, the system of online performance metrics was found to be extensive and implemented well within the strategic reasoning context.

Another aspect of the ratio category we rated, was the availability and use of an overall strategic navigational model. In this area, we found indications of a good start and see potential for a quick extension to a complete navigational model.

Our market observations do strengthen our belief in the need for such a system, yet very few companies are currently found to have a strong overall navigational model in place.

Overall strategy and future opportunities

Visualising getmobile.de's value chain landscape of today, we can come up with Figure 4.3.8.

Having initially started with a mobile phone retail shop on the Internet, the company by now has integrated backward and forward elements of the value chain. The forward integration was done through the cardmaxx.de initiative, while the backward integration was achieved through the WAP Telecom acquisition. In addition to this B2C offering, a B2B spot market offering was presented through the tel2bmarket.net initiative. The last move to be noted was a diagonalisation to offering a hosted shop for Motorola.de.

Through applying the e-roadmapping analysis a number of sensible future opportunities emerged; the results of which we clustered in the following three categories.

1. *After sales for contract customers*

The most obvious and easiest to achieve is an after-sales service offering for the B2C contract customers. The German mobile telephone market is characterised through service contracts of typically a two-year duration. This does not provide the retailer with frequent repeat customer interactions. For the prepaid

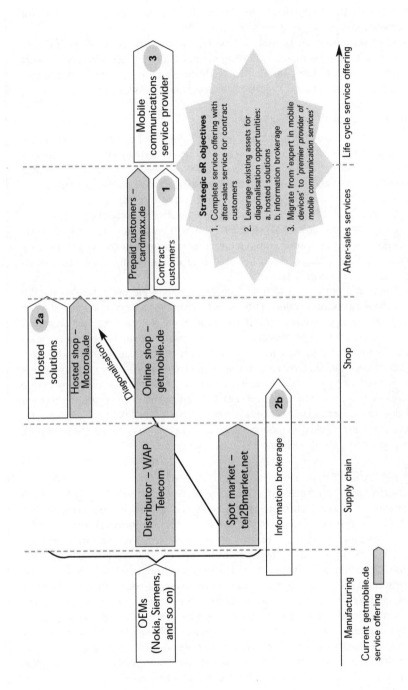

Figure 4.3.8 getmobile.de's value chain and future opportunities

Strategic eR objectives

1. Complete service offering with after-sales service for contract customers
2. Leverage existing assets for diagonalisation opportunities:
   a. hosted solutions
   b. information brokerage
3. Migrate from 'expert in mobile devices' to *premier provider of mobile communication services*'

OEMs (Nokia, Siemens, and so on)

Distributor – WAP Telecom

Spot market – tel2Bmarket.net

Information brokerage

Online shop – getmobile.de

Hosted shop – Motorola.de

Hosted solutions

Diagonalisation

Prepaid customers – cardmaxx.de

Contract customers

Mobile communications service provider

Current getmobile.de service offering

Manufacturing   Supply chain   Shop   After-sales services   Life cycle service offering

1   2a   2b   3

customers, the cardmaxx.de service closes this strategic gap and puts the company periodically in touch with the customers.

Contract customers as well have needs for after-sales service, which can be met in a systematic manner, affording getmobile.de a closer and more continuous contact with the customer, leading to future repeat purchases of the core product offering through a more intimate customer relationship.

2. *Leveraging diagonalisation opportunities*

The second strategic opportunity lies within further initiatives to leverage the existing asset base. A fine example of a successful early move is the offering of the hosted shop for Motorola.de. Through the availability of a complete mobile telephony shop and a close relationship developed through the tel2bmarket.net unit, a complete diagonal offering was made available to Motorola.

Further diagonalisation efforts seem very feasible in the area of hosted solutions in the 'shop' value chain element. This could entail shops for manufacturers and/or distributors in their communication with partners further down the value chain (B2B). Or shops could be integrated in, for example, various lifestyle portals, and so on (B2C).

Crossing over the manufacturing, supply chain and shop value chain elements, a second diagonalisation offering becomes feasible: information brokerage. Through involvement in three elements of the value chain, a wide range of behavioural data becomes available. Particularly, the information gained at the spot market unit seems fit for tactical use of manufacturers. Provided enough liquidity is passing over the tel2bmarket.net, manufacturers could use this data to confirm indications of model shortages of competitors, allowing subsequent aggressive marketing of their own similar product. Or manufacturers can utilise this marketplace for reasons of observing price erosion. These data would not allow predictive usage, yet would give the manufacturers great insights into the speed of price erosion across the model range.

3. *Migration to service provider*

The third and most long-term-oriented opportunity lies with the migration from an Internet product retailer to an Internet-based service provider company. We saw in the first opportunity (after sales for contract customers) that an extension of a product offering – particularly in a low-interval repeat market, like the German mobile market – towards services can be achieved fairly easily. Yet the main opportunity lies within the migration away from product selling to a life-cycle service offering. A unique opportunity exists for getmobile.de to become the premier provider of mobile communication services for its customers. For example, could not customers be retained by availing them the 'one view' on their communication expenses and behaviour? If getmobile.de were to offer their customers this integrated view of all telephony bills, including a periodical analysis of usage pattern and recommendation of more adequate providers, plus maybe even a payment platform, this would surely tie the customer to the company. Services like the aforementioned can be designed in manifold ways around the various customer needs. These services have to be profitable and need to be a strong differentiating advantage. Yet, this seems a viable road to profitable survival in a continuously margin-reducing commodity market.

In conclusion, our eRI analysis detailed the major four pillars of the company with a particular focus on value metrics, while an e-roadmapping analysis showed some promising future opportunities.

References

Kehoe, C.F. (2000) M-commerce: Advantage, Europe. *The McKinsey Quarterly*, (2): 43–5.

Peet, J. (2000) Distribution dilemmas. *The Economist*, **8159**: 25–30.

GoIndustry.com: Surplus Equipment Online

Paul Vega, Business Development Group, GoIndustry.com

CHAPTER CONTENTS

Introduction

In April 1999, GoIndustry.com was founded by two former consultants and a venture capitalist to create a B2B trading platform for used and surplus equipment. The company received its first round of financing of US$10 million from Atlas Venture in October 1999, and launched its website in December 1999. The second round of financing of over 42 million euros closed in May 2000, with Internet Capital Group and Atlas Venture as lead investors. The headquarters of this e-commerce start-up are located in Munich, Germany with main offices in London and Paris, and additional subsidiaries across Europe. GoIndustry's mission is to become *the* leading asset recovery service provider online with the full range of value-added services and offline capabilities. With regards to the latter, GoIndustry has just completed the strategic acquisition of Karner & Co. AG auctioneers to complete the offline market offering.

GoIndustry is perceived by many industry analysts as the most successful first mover in Europe, and has been ranked the number one start-up in

Germany by the Handelsblatt's e-business publication, and rated among the top four start-ups by the consultancy Bain & Company and *Focus Money* magazine.[1] This contribution aims to depict the development path of GoIndustry's business model, strategy and implementation approach.

Why focus on business-to-business?

At the highest level of analysis, research focusing on the Internet will have to differentiate between B2B and B2C online markets. Until very recently, most investors, entrepreneurs, and journalists have focused on relatively successful B2C companies such as Amazon.com, E*TRADE, and eToys. Ironically, more recently the media's attention has been drawn to high-profile B2C failures such as Boo.com, Reel.com, and Clickmango. Consequently, many experts now agree that the largest share of e-commerce value and growth will be in what Merill Lynch has termed 'the Internet's next frontier: B2B e-commerce'.[2]

As shown in Table 4.4.1, B2C is characterised by lower average transaction values with shorter-term, and less formalised commercial relationships. Moreover, B2C is far more advertising intensive as it targets a

Table 4.4.1   Comparing B2B and B2C characteristics

	Business-to-Business	Business-to-Consumer
Transaction size	Average US$75,000	Average US$75
Participants	Multiple companies and employees	Consumer direct to merchant
Pricing	Negotiated, contracts, auctions, catalogue	Mainly catalogue, fixed price
Decision makers	Approvals needed; business rules govern	Single consumer
Procurement catalyst	Demand chain driven for direct procurement; replenishment for indirect	Impulse, casual purchase, advertisement, word of mouth
Selection criteria	Value, partnership, or equity driven	Brand driven, price sensitive, advertising
Fulfilment perspective	Availability and fulfilment details more important	Lenient on fulfilment, more likely to wait for backorder product
Credit	Credit cards, sophisticated systems on the way, for example Identrus digital signatures, e-escrow, and so on	All consumer credit cards, cash on delivery
Infrastructure	Local, customised catalogue; workflow rules	Browser with Internet access

Source: Merill Lynch (2000), GoIndustry.com, and own research

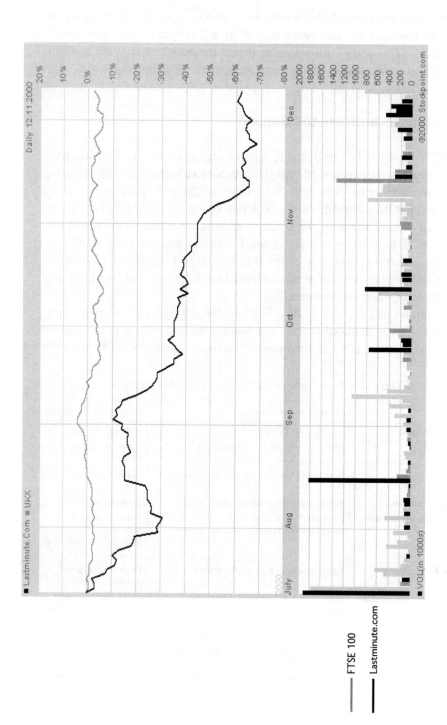

Figure 4.4.1 B2C Lastminute.com stock price vs. FTSE 100[3]

FTSE 100

Lastminute.com

broader base of potential customers. Lastminute.com, for example, spent millions in promotion and marketing leading up to its IPO, only to see its share price fall as investors turned elsewhere (Figure 4.4.1).

Many terms have been used to describe the new B2B business models, for example dynamic trading hubs, market makers, electronic marketplaces, infomediaries, online trading communities, web intermediaries, vertical portals, and so on. In this context, B2B e-commerce is defined as commerce conducted between businesses over the Internet, extranet, or intranet.[4] B2B e-commerce may also be conducted directly between buyers and sellers or through a third party, who will be referred to as an online intermediary. This contribution will specifically focus on online B2B auctions and dynamic pricing trading platforms such as GoIndustry, Dovebid, and Tradeout. Market makers such as GoIndustry.com aim to match buyers and sellers more efficiently both in vertical markets, such as construction and agriculture, and in horizontal markets for MRO, and industrial equipment (Figure 4.4.2).

In terms of the number of Internet firms taking part in this aggressive 'land grab', Berlecon Research counted close to 1100 B2B start-ups in August 2000, and the Gartner Group believe that this number will quadruple to more than 4000 companies by 2004.[5] Also, from a financial perspective, the stakes of B2B remain high. The Gartner Group predict a market volume of US$7.29 trillion by 2004, and even the relatively conservative Merrill Lynch's and Goldman Sachs' estimates of US$2.5 trillion and US$1.5 trillion respectively are impressive.[6] Optimism and investor

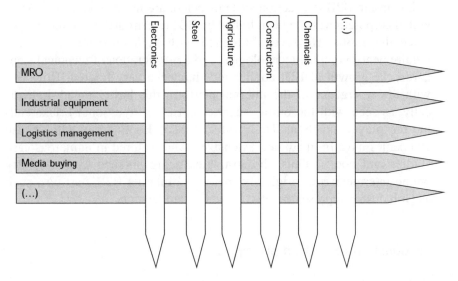

Figure 4.4.2   Vertical and horizontal markets (illustrative example)

Table 4.4.2   Stock market valuations of selected B2B companies

Company	Ticker	Stock Price US$	LTM revs. ($000)	Shares (000)	Enterprise Value ($000)	EV/LTM Market Multiple
B2B ONLINE MARKETPLACES						
Freemarkets	FMKT	54.50	43,380	37,580	2,048,110	**47**
Sciquest	SQST	8.56	20,924	29,000	248,240	**12**
Ventro	VNTR	12.56	76,289	45,640	573,238	**8**
VerticalNet	VERT	47.87	96,282	86,100	4,121,607	**43**
B2B TECHNOLOGY PROVIDERS						
Ariba	ARBA	144.87	161,327	240,620	34,858,619	**216**
Commerce One	CMRC	50.43	124,964	162,000	8,169,660	**65**
I2 Technologies	ITWO	152.00	750,465	198,120	30,114,240	**40**

1. Stock price: quoted on 24 August 2000. *Source:* Yahoo.com Finance and Free Edgar online
2. LTM revenues: Last 12 months revenues from Jun 99–Jun 00, calculated from 10-Q, 10-K SEC reports
3. EV: Enterprise Value is stock market cap. based on shares outstanding multiplied by stock price
4. EV/LTM: Multiple of market cap. over earnings. P/E ratio analysis is not suitable for Internet companies

confidence in online B2B start-ups are also reflected in the highly exuberant stock market valuations and earnings multiples. Even after the NASDAQ stock market crash of April 2000, companies such as B2B technology provider Ariba and auction platform Freemarkets are valued at over 200 and over 40 times their respective last 12 month (LTM) revenues.[7]

Electronic B2B transaction systems per se are not new concepts. Most global corporations have been linked by EDI (electronic data interchange) since the 1980s. However, burdened with high up-front investment requirements, complex technologies, and a proliferation of technical standards, the growth of EDI applications has been very limited. However, with the emergence of the Internet platform this has changed dramatically, as seen with the online success stories of traditional bricks-and-mortar players such as Dell, Intel, Cisco, FedEx, and GE. These companies have been studied extensively and featured in numerous case studies and books. Thus, the strategies being pursued by third-party online intermediaries, originally 'pureplay' Internet B2B start-ups, such as GoIndustry, represent relatively 'uncharted territory'.

Introduction to auction principles

To fully understand the value add of online business models it is useful to first have a look at the offline market characteristics and established value chains. The auction transaction model is one of the most versatile and sophisticated transaction mechanisms serving sellers, buyers, and market needs. It has also been a very popular tool used by governments, as seen with the US radio spectrum auctions or with the more recent third generation wireless network licence auctions in the UK and Germany. By definition in this context, an auction is a regulated and formalised method for allocating scarce resources, based upon price competition, where a seller wishes to maximise his disposal price and where a buyer wishes to spend as little as possible. In ascending (English) auctions, price and allocation are determined in an open bidding competition. The bidders willing to pay the highest price win.

The following sections will centre around the overall market structure of B2B auctions, in particular the market for used and surplus industrial assets. The auction business for surplus equipment was chosen for this case study because it provides a good cross-section of vertical industry groups such as construction and automotive, as well as horizontal asset classes such as office equipment and machine tools. Surplus and idle assets are often targeted by the new generation of B2B auction start-ups based on a very large market opportunity and the inherent inefficiencies of the offline auction market. Thus, this section provides a detailed overview of the offline auction value chain from the following perspectives: industry structure and geographical spread, price determination and transaction costs, asymmetric product and pricing information. This dissection of the offline auction market will serve to highlight the benefits of online business models that will be introduced in the case study featured on GoIndustry.com.

Industry structure

Independent pureplay online B2B auction start-ups have valid reasons to target niche segments of fragmented and inefficient offline markets (Figure 4.4.3). Buyers and sellers in the fragmented offline B2B markets, have interacted and done business with one another in the same way for decades via dispersed auction houses, brokers, and commission intermediaries. The process of identifying, qualifying, contacting, and transacting with the most appropriate trading partners has been limited to fax, phone, mail, exhibitions, and trade fairs.

In GoIndustry.com's market for used and surplus assets for example, the offline market is controlled by a multi-channel distribution network, dominated by dealers, brokers, and commission intermediaries. In other words, equipment very rarely travels directly from end-user sellers to end-user

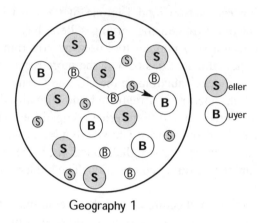

Geography 1

Figure 4.4.3   Fragmented domestic auction market

buyers. In practice, end-user sellers often do not have the expertise, resources, or contacts to dispose of their assets efficiently. Likewise, procurement officers on the buy side have limited visibility of the supplier market and little basis for broad comparisons between different products, different suppliers, or across different countries. The market is not transparent and is difficult to segment. There are also many commission brokers who add little value to the transaction process or to the products per se apart from sourcing the next buy-side customer.

Moreover, there is no single auctioneer who controls any dominant share of any domestic market or the pan-European market for that matter. End users, dealers, and brokers of industrial equipment have traditionally been restricted to expensive local marketing campaigns and resource-intensive sales calls to find buyers. In contrast to Sotheby's and Christie's global dominance of consumer auctions for arts and collectibles, only a few offline B2B auction houses have international sales operations. Offline auctions of idle assets are currently executed by a fragmented and primarily regional group of auctioneers. Even top European players in this field are far from having a dominant market share in any single country market. Many offline cross-border transactions are conducted on an ad hoc basis through loose partnerships and personal contacts in overseas markets. This fragmentation applies not only to the auctioneers per se, but also to the B2B industry sectors which are served by auctioneers. In chemicals, construction, electronics, metals, and plastics, for example, the top five players hold less than 20 per cent market share (Table 4.4.3).

Table 4.4.3 Indicators of fragmentation in various industries[8]

	FRAGMENTATION INDICATORS			
Industry	Top 5 companies % of sales	Rank	# of Estab. ('000)	Rank
Aerospace	46.1	11	150	4
Chemicals	16.6	7	13	11
Construction	1.8	1	650	1
Electronics	13.1	6	24	8
Food	4.6	2	176	3
Forest/Paper	27.0	9	6	12
Healthcare	10.6	4	646	2
Metals	8.1	3	68	6
Automotive	35.3	10	123	5
Plastics	12.4	5	17	9
Telecom	63.1	12	30	7
Utilities	20.0	8	15	10

Source: US Department of Commerce statistics 1999, CSFB Analysis

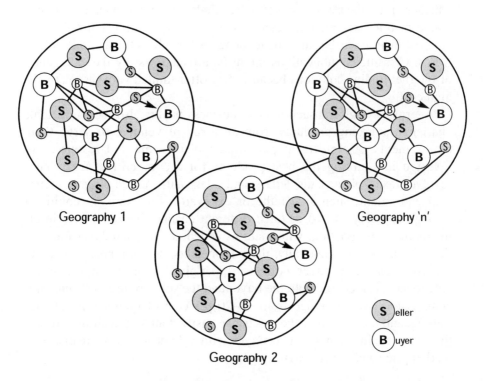

Geography 1

Geography 'n'

Geography 2

S eller

B uyer

Figure 4.4.4 Fragmented auction markets with geographical clusters

The fragmentation of markets in offline B2B is further exacerbated by geographical limitations and boundaries (Figure 4.4.4). The cross-border European secondary market is not as well developed as in the US due to international tax issues, different languages, multiple currencies, health and safety regulations, and other international complications. Thus, the auction business has traditionally been very localised, based on word of mouth, and personal relationships developed at exhibitions and trade fairs.

Price setting and transaction costs

In the offline world, pricing mechanisms are very complex and inefficient, and transaction costs are extremely high. End-user sellers, for example, have had to deal with certain dealers and brokers that buy their assets at a fraction of their value. Classifieds on the other hand, list guide prices in their ads and, therefore, sellers cannot force an outcome that matches them to a buyer on the right side of the distribution curve. Moreover, classified ads are static, limited in circulation, and generate cost whether or not the assets are sold. Classifieds effectively anchor the upper bound of price negotiations, and do not allow sellers to capture the true value of their assets because the tendency is for sellers to negotiate downwards. Classifieds publications might be affected first by the emergence of Internet trading solutions because they offer limited value at relatively high cost.

In terms of high transaction cost, business buyers also face a difficult challenge sourcing products from an array of vendors to serve their requirements. A significant part of a buyer's time and resources is invested in sourcing the best products for a competitive price. This involves faxes, phone calls, letters, and sales visits. A used piece of industrial equipment, such as a lathe or excavator, for example, could go through as many as two or three different channel intermediaries in an international transaction, with margins added at every handover transaction (Figure 4.4.5). Generally, the intermediary or auctioneer who finds the final end-user buyer collects the highest transaction premium. Auctioneers can charge both the buyer and the seller of used equipment a commission that can range from 10–20 per cent of transaction volume. Subsequently, the price of the assets can easily double, travelling through the value chain from seller to buyer with sellers unable to realise fair market price and buyers paying high fees.

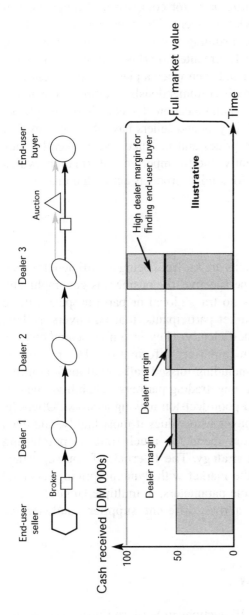

Figure 4.4.5 Margin structures and inefficient transactions in B2B auctions

Product and market information

Without the Internet to assist, market participants have poor access to relevant product information and little basis for comparison. Equipment and materials are often sold ex-works 'as seen'. The previous sections have shown how difficult and time-consuming it can be in offline markets to match buyers and sellers in a fragmented market. Moreover, product descriptions are not standardised and even when a piece of equipment is of the same make and model, it can differ tremendously in terms of condition, wear and tear. Given inefficient communication channels driven by phone, fax, catalogue and so on, not all buyers and sellers have the same level of detailed information on current prices and products. Subsequently, they cannot determine prices efficiently due to imperfect information, which explains high price differentials for similar products across the market.

Resulting inefficiencies

As one can deduce, offline auctions are far from being an efficient transaction channel. From a structural perspective, the business is geographically dispersed and currently there is no truly global or pan-European offline auctioneer. Furthermore, all market participants, that is, buyers, sellers, and auctioneers, operate very inefficiently. They face high search costs in the offline world coupled with imperfect information. The process is further rife with inefficiencies including missed calls, malfunctioning fax machines, and uncertainty about new trading partners' reliability. The end result is wasted time at best and poor decision making at worst. Often the product is not matched to the buyer who values it most highly, and even worse, business decision makers spend too much time on purchasing decisions instead of sales and strategy. The Internet, of course, brings powerful new search tools to the market with dynamic pricing, detailed product descriptions with multiple parameters, in multiple languages, and almost instant comparability across different suppliers and service providers on a global basis.

The B2B auction opportunity

The total transaction value of B2B auctions in Western Europe is expected to grow from US$1.6 billion in 1998 to an estimated US$54.0 billion in 2002. This implies a four-year compounded annual growth rate (CAGR)

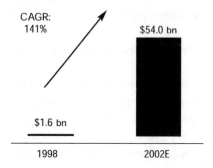

Figure 4.4.6   Western European B2B Internet auctions
(Keenan Vision Oct. 1998)

of 141 per cent, which is one of the highest expected growth rates in the Internet space (Figure 4.4.6). Forrester Research stresses the fact that companies will increasingly use dynamic pricing to determine valuations for products and services and thus products will be more efficiently allocated among buyers. Forrester points out that standard, well-understood dynamic pricing formats, especially auctions, will dominate as they afford maximum benefits to both buyers and sellers.

Vernon Keenan of Keenan Vision commented:

> By 2002, 29% of all Internet economy transactions will be performed on exchanges [dynamic pricing or auction technology portals].

Whit Andrews of Internet World (29 March 1999, *Integrating Auctions into Everyday Business*), added that:

> many [merchandisers] are being forced to think beyond the idea of auctions as a mistake-fixer for those times when they overstock an item. They are looking at auctions as a critical part of their everyday business.

The business model of GoIndustry

GoIndustry is a new Internet company with an ambitious strategy to create a multi-industry business-to-business (B2B) Internet trading platform in Europe (Figure 4.4.7). Revenues will primarily be derived from commissions for successful facilitation of dynamic and fixed-priced auctions (both offline and online) for surplus inventory and used assets. GoIndustry's key to success and core value proposition is a robust transaction-enabling infrastructure.

This transaction-enabling infrastructure has several primary components:

1. Sell-side development: GoIndustry industry-veteran sales force rapidly sources equipment from blue chip companies, SMEs (small and medium-sized enterprises), liquidators, and leasing companies. 'Sales force' has a slightly counter-intuitive meaning in this context, as this implies sales people promoting the GoIndustry concept to suppliers and uploading their assets to the website. Deep choice and liquidity attract buyers.

2. Buy-side development: This entails an aggressive, pan-European marketing strategy. Driving buy-side traffic is key to achieving rapid sell-through of auction items. 'Transaction is our religion' is a maxim often repeated by GoIndustry management. Marketing leverages online banner-ads, affiliate programs, and cross-links to other relevant horizontal and vertical websites and portals. Offline marketing targets the trade press, specialist publications and equipment classifieds.

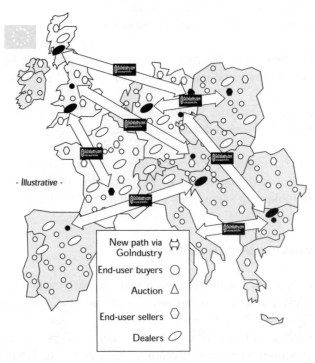

Figure 4.4.7   The GoIndustry trading platform concept

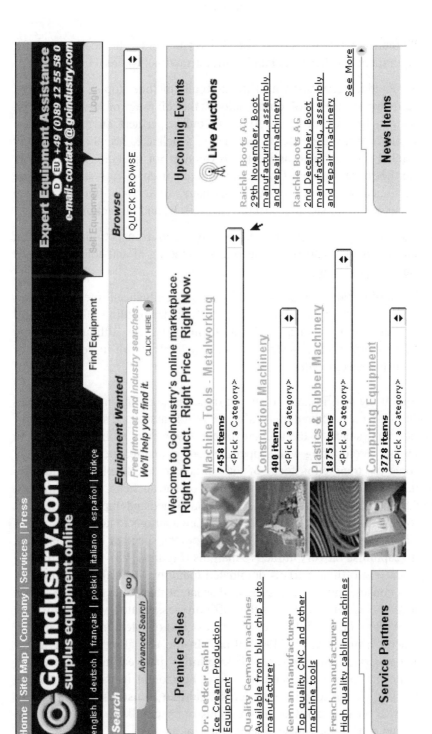

Figure 4.4.8 Multi-lingual, multi-currency trading platform

GoIndustry also has a team of 'market makers' who seek buyers for equipment and facilitate hand-held transactions where required.

3. Value-added services: Under the umbrella of 'one-stop shop' industrial recovery services, GoIndustry delivers the full range of services through partnerships with leading offline and online partners, such as Deutsche Bank (secure online escrow payments), Kuehne & Nagel and Schenker (global logistics with online RFQs (request for quotation)), and so on. Furthermore, through GoIndustry's acquisition of full-service offline auctioneer Karner & Co. AG in Germany, the service offering has been expanded to on-site live auctions, appraisals, and inspections.

4. Function-specific process knowledge and transaction facilitation know-how developed by a deep understanding of and consistent focus on market making.

5. Technological strength enabled by the most advanced Internet transaction technology available. The GoIndustry trading platform will primarily consist of a single, multi-industry site, although strategic partnerships with industry players will likely result in co-branded or industry-specific sites.

GoIndustry will initially focus on dynamic auctions and e-commerce-enabled classifieds of predominantly used or idle assets and surplus inventory that are well suited to the auction format. Over time, GoIndustry plans to enrich this core offering with supporting content and features that decisively reinforce the transaction focus of the GoIndustry marketplace. So far, this includes asset and stock management tools, on-site auctions, and live webcast auctions, which have all been successfully launched and implemented.

GoIndustry has chosen to start with online auctions to take advantage of gaps in competitive offerings, to benefit from the speed of implementation, and to capitalise on very attractive margins (Figure 4.4.8). GoIndustry will target current offline markets dominated today by low value-add brokers, auction houses, and trade press as well as latent sales of assets often left on balance sheets simply due to the difficulty associated with liquidating them. Worldwide, the idle asset and excess and obsolete inventory market has been estimated at US$350 billion.[9] In the UK alone, the classifieds market generates approximately US$5 billion[10] per year in revenues.

While the primary GoIndustry site is horizontal in nature, providing similar transaction functionality across multiple industry segments, GoIndustry will move quickly to secure industry-specific knowledge, relationships, and staff to maximise asset and inventory sales.

Summary of GoIndustry's benefits to buyers and sellers

▓ *Reduces transaction/acquisition costs.* The offline costs associated with negotiating a deal for items of considerable value can be significant. The online marketplace allows two parties in a transaction to find the other faster and less expensively.

▓ *Permits costs to be contingent upon the success of the sale.* One-way media, such as classifieds, do not provide the functionality to track the success of published ads and effectively invoice for them.

▓ *Maximises the potential for the seller to find the buyer with the highest valuation.* This implies that by using an online, liquid marketplace, any seller (end user or dealer) has a higher chance of realising the maximum price for that particular item.

▓ *Eliminates multi-intermediary transactions.* With the existence of an online liquid market-making place, the number of inter-intermediary transactions will fall dramatically.

▓ *Maximises the potential for the buyer to find exactly what he or she is looking for.* Buyers (or brokers working on their behalf) will be able to see a large selection of the relevant items that are for sale that fit the buyer's requirements.

The combined benefits are shared between both buyers and sellers in any given transaction. Buyers see inventory from multiple sellers and choose which offering to bid for. Consequently, buyers have a better sense of the fair market value of products in addition to a lower cost of procurement. On the other hand, sellers can circumvent much of the costly intermediation landscape. They can contact a broader field of buyers and elicit the largest possible number of competitive bids for their product. This manifests itself in a higher price for their goods. While GoIndustry offers clear value to both buyer and seller, it is principally aligned with the seller. Over time, GoIndustry expects the seller to be able to extract more consumer surplus from the buyers than was the case before. This value proposition is consistent with driving the revenue model driven by seller commissions.

Categorisation and roll-out approach

Given finite resources to apply against a broad array of industry sectors, segment prioritisation is critical. Furthermore, given GoIndustry's know-

ledge base and potential threat of incumbent participants, it is a fundamental part of GoIndustry's strategy to expand its industry expertise.
GoIndustry will address these points through a straightforward strategy of
segment selection, strategy development, and execution. Vertical selection
will be determined based primarily upon market size, strong potential for
development of a pan-European market, existence of a market for asset
resale and surplus inventory liquidation, and appropriateness of the goods
traded for Internet auction transactions. The specific strategy adopted will
depend upon the dynamics of the industry in question. The execution will
include drawing upon industry-specific expertise by hiring a sales staff,
retaining well-connected market makers, forging partnerships, and
selecting knowledgeable advisers and board members.

Competitive factors

It is important to underscore that to date there is no comparable online
service with full offline capabilities in operation in Europe. GoIndustry
recognises that this aberration will be corrected. The company is also
cognizant that the lag between US launch and successful EU replication
or expansion will not offer the two- to three-year lead time for development which was afforded to B2C companies. However, GoIndustry is
confident that through rapid and immediate action it can take advantage
of the immense B2B opportunities in Europe. Further, through aggressive
and rapid execution GoIndustry will create significant, sustainable
competitive advantage in a market with high switching costs and significant network externalities. Key potential competitors fall into the
following categories: auction-based market-making portals, online classifieds, single-industry Internet verticals, auction houses and brokers
migrating to the Internet, trade magazines, and consumer-focused hori-
zontals with business offerings. GoIndustry believes that it has significant
advantages enabling GoIndustry to compete with each effectively. GoIndustry is the first mover in both Germany and the UK to execute this arbi-
trage model, providing an advantage versus other potential auction-based
market-making portals. Compared to offline classifieds, GoIndustry
wields the power of dynamic pricing along with a large sales force and
highly focused marketing campaign.

Compared to single-industry Internet verticals, GoIndustry brings functional expertise including intimacy with the entire process of executing
B2B auctions including management of a direct sales force, ability to
market a clear message and value proposition to the appropriate decision

maker within each organisation, provision of the most advanced auction technology, and partnerships with transaction facilitating service providers. Furthermore, GoIndustry will be the first mover to develop a critical mass of these items, creating a competitive advantage as eBay has done across categories in the consumer space. Compared to offline auction houses, GoIndustry does not face channel conflict – a factor which makes dealers reluctant to work with offline auction houses today.

Strategy and the road ahead

Industry prioritisation and adoption rates

The following sections examine theoretical frameworks that help companies, such as GoIndustry, identify high potential markets and develop effective growth strategies. There is a wide range of theories and approaches to growth strategies and critical success factors of B2B Internet markets. Some studies of comparative nature draw conclusions from differences between electronic and traditional offline markets, whereas others analyse endogenous behaviour within electronic markets. This chapter will now focus on two specific dimensions within online B2B marketplaces:

1. *Adoption rates and asset class prioritisation:* In other words, which asset classes or industries have the highest potential to benefit from online B2B marketplaces? Which industries or industrial asset classes would most likely adopt new technologies and Internet applications?

2. *Network externalities and market entry barriers:* In other words, how can a B2B marketplace rapidly scale its business model through Internet and community interconnectivity? What drives aggressive growth and expansion strategies of B2B marketplaces?

Turning to (1), the adoption of technologies follows an 'S-curve' (Figure 4.4.9). In its early stages there are few users – the flat part at the bottom of the 'S'. Then, as adoption reaches a critical level, the user base grows so quickly that the growth rate is nearly vertical. The rapid growth occurs as a result of the virtuous cycle that is generated at this critical junction. Enough people are using the technology such that the utility of using it increases rapidly and drives adoption at a very steep rate (network effects); meanwhile, the influx of new users yet again increases the development of applications or useful content, thus increasing the utility of the technology further.

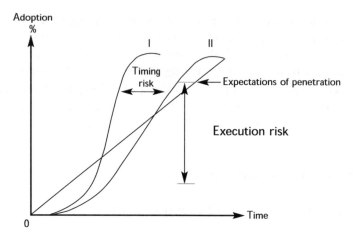

Figure 4.4.9   Market adoption with risks

The part of the 'S-curve' at which adoption increases exponentially is called the point of inflection. Arguably, that point of inflection for the Internet is occurring in Europe today and its impact will be far reaching. For some technologies it has taken decades to evolve from a new technology on the flat bottom part of the curve to becoming a ubiquitous component in every office. Telex or fax machines are examples of technologies which took years to get to the top of the curve, but they have become essential for every business. In contrast, the Internet is achieving this feat at an unprecedented rate due to its sheer utility. Networking externalities and the factors that drive them will be explained in more detail in the following sub-section. Adoption rates and the build-up of critical mass on the buy side and sell side are crucial for a B2B marketplace. Thus, prioritising the right industry sectors is crucial to a start-up's success. Which industries would most likely take up online B2B applications?

Building on analyses of CSFB and others, research has identified industry clusters that are exceptionally well suited for market penetration by B2B auction houses or B2B marketplaces in general.[11] In particular, four key variable factors drive adoption rates in the B2B space:

1. *Offline market fragmentation:* How many of the big competitors control what percentage of total market share? What is the level of concentration?

2. *Rate of IT adoption:* Are the buyers and sellers already online? What is the level of IT investment?

Table 4.4.4   Predictors of B2B adoption[12]

Industry	FRAGMENTATION INDICATORS Top 5 % of sales	Rank	# of estab. (000s)	Rank	COST STRUCTURE SG&A % of sales	Rank	PROFIT STRUCTURE Net margin %	Rank	RETURNS PROFILE RONA %	Rank	IT ADOPTION IT $ as % sales	Rank	ASSET INTENSITY Sales/ assets	Rank
Aerospace	46.1	11	150	4	11.5	11	3.8	5	4.1	7	4.5	3	1.1	12
Banks	–	–	–	–	25.7	1	15.6	15	1.4	1	5.8	1	0.1	1
Chemicals	16.6	7	13	11	16.7	5	10.5	13	7.5	14	2.0	11	0.7	6
Construction	1.8	1	650	1	13.6	10	6.5	12	6.6	12	0.9	15	0.9	11
Electronics	13.1	6	24	8	13.7	9	5.3	10	5.7	10	3.2	6	1.1	13
Food	4.6	2	176	3	16.0	6	4.0	6	7.2	13	1.8	13	1.7	15
Pulp/Paper	27.0	9	6	12	20.4	3	4.8	9	4.5	8	2.0	12	0.9	9
Machinery	–	–	NA	–	15.0	8	3.6	4	10.1	15	2.4	10	1.4	14
Metals	8.1	3	68	6	5.8	13	2.3	1	2.5	2	1.2	14	0.9	10
Automotive	35.3	10	123	5	9.0	12	3.4	3	3.4	6	3.0	7	0.7	4
Plastics	12.4	5	17	9	15.1	7	2.6	2	2.7	3	2.5	9	0.8	7
Telecom	63.1	12	30	7	21.0	2	12.3	14	6.2	11	5.2	2	0.5	3

Source: CSFB Analysis, US Department of Commerce

3. *Profit structure:* Do marketplaces realise high margins in this sector?

4. *Asset intensity:* Is this an industry or asset class with high turnover in capital equipment? What is the utilisation level of assets in this industry?

Common sense would suggest that buyers and sellers traditionally operating in highly fragmented industries could realise and unlock substantial value from participating in online B2B marketplaces, leading to high adoption rates. However, companies operating in such fragmented offline markets can also display backward, paper-based workflows, manual processes, and a low understanding of Internet technologies, exacerbated by conservative management teams who are used to doing things 'the old way'. This is particularly true for the offline auction business analysed in this sub-chapter. Lacking dominant offline players in the market, there are fewer companies with the resources or incentives to adopt world-class technologies and Internet applications. Thus, while fragmentation is a good indicator of the long-term degree (potential) of online B2B adoption, it is by no means correlated to the speed at which these solutions are adopted or implemented (Table 4.4.4). With incumbent auctioneers in the offline world slow to capture online market opportunities, independent pureplay Internet start-ups can move quickly to establish first mover advantages.

In order to qualify the overall online B2B adoption rate potential of individual industries, one could refer to Table 4.4.4. Selected industries are ranked according to the criteria outlined earlier: (a) degree of fragmentation, (b) cost structure, that is, SG & A (sales, general and administration) to sales, (c) profitability, (d) returns profile, (e) IT spend, (f) fixed asset and working capital intensity.

Network externalities and systems dynamics

In this battle, winners often take all. B2B may be like financial markets in which a single exchange tends to win most trading and profits, even if it is not the best. If a second-rate exchange is first to attract a critical mass of trading, even a better trading system may fail to wrest business away (*The Economist*, 1 April 2000)

Connecting the maximum number of buyers and sellers is of fundamental importance in creating a liquid B2B marketplace. A recent A.T. Kearney survey interviewed more than 100 B2B e-hubs and nearly all cited critical mass and deep industry expertise as critical success factors.[13] This is based on the assumption that some goods and services generate more value when more users consume the same goods and services. The consumers using these products constitute networks in which the utility derived from consumption of these goods or services increases as additional consumers purchase the same goods and services.

A market characterised by such properties is called a network market in which there are positive consumption externalities termed network externalities. These network effects are in stark contrast to the zero-sum or scarcity models because market participants derive more value from the market as the number of participants increases. For instance, mobile phone WAP technology adds more value if there is a large installed base of WAP users who can send and receive data in WAP format. In terms of B2B auction companies there needs to be a large number of sell-side products available for sale coupled with high buy-side demand.

The Internet networking model or Metcalfe's Law (named after Bob Metcalfe, the designer of the Ethernet and founder of 3Com) states that the value of a network equals the square of the number of network members. This implies that if you develop a network where any member can transact with another member, the number of potential connections each of the N-members can make is $(N-1)$, giving a total number of potential connections as $N(N-1)$ or N^2-N. Assuming each potential connection is worth as much as any other, the value to each user depends on the total size of the network, and the total value of potential connectivity scales much faster than the size of the network, proportional to N^2. Direct network externalities are generated through the direct effects of the number of agents consuming the same product or service. This underlines the challenge facing all B2B Internet start-ups today and it is particularly difficult to do for used or surplus B2B products. Since idle assets and excess inventory are reasonably unique, there is no continuous supply curve. Networking effects created by matching buyers and sellers in the surplus auction business are more difficult to achieve because products are not very homogeneous and not readily available through known sales channels. This dramatically compounds the problem of creating links between as many buyers and sellers as possible, since the probability of creating a match between a buyer and a seller for a particular item is a positive function of the number of links that are created between transacting parties.

As described in previous sections, this problem has been addressed to date by offline intermediary networks including dealers, brokers, and classifieds. These intermediary landscapes can be complex with dealers, brokers, and classifieds trying to provide the bridges between sellers and buyers who would never be able to find each other without the offline intermediary network. In the online world, matching across borders and also across industries has been the strategy to solve this problem. Office equipment and PCs for example find their use in almost any industry and by connection of different industry network communities on one platform, a company like GoIndustry can leverage cross-network effects. Another benefit of the Internet is of course geographical scaling. GoIndustry, for example, networks country markets on a global basis through a multi-lingual, multi-currency transaction platform. Lastly, GoIndustry can now match the offline capabilities and network of its traditional competitors through the acquisition of offline auctioneer Karner AG in Germany. Some economists interpret critical mass as the so-called 'chicken and egg' paradox from observations that a network size is too small to induce consumers into the network. In turn, because no consumers are willing to join the network, the expected size of the network remains small. In the context of B2B marketplaces, the 'Catch 22' lies in the fact that buyers will not be drawn to a B2B website without sellers, and sellers will not join the network without strong buy-side demand.

Descriptive case studies, like the one presented on GoIndustry, cannot fully structure dynamic complexity to explain critical mass growth strategies. Thus, systems dynamics (SD) theory can provide a useful framework to analyse B2B market dynamics and network externalities based on the notion of feedback loops and reinforcing network effects. SD can organise and structure descriptive information, retain key aspects of real processes, build on the experience of the modelling participants, and map different policy scenarios by input and outcome factors. As illustrated in the SD model (Figure 4.4.10) B2B marketplaces and auction houses have to develop aggressive strategies to overcome the 'chicken and egg' dilemma. Should a B2B marketplace drive critical mass on the buy side to attract suppliers first or vice versa? A generic model of a B2B market-place is displayed in Figure 4.4.10. This reinforcing loop shows how buy-side critical mass drives sell-side critical mass to an Internet platform and vice versa.

Taking it one step further, a systems dynamics model can also show at which points a B2B marketplace can intervene to encourage the creation of networking effects. To attract buyers, for example, GoIndustry spends a substantial amount on focused advertising in the trade press and online media. Buy-side traffic is also driven by partnerships with the leading online portals and communities in the respective asset classes. As the

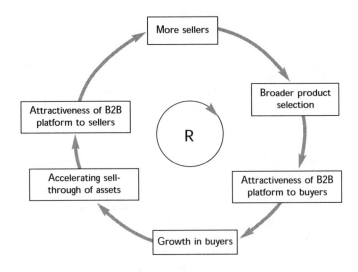

Figure 4.4.10   Online B2B network effects in an SD model

buyer group grows, it attracts sellers who are drawn by the promise of high sell-through rates and higher prices.

On the sell side, GoIndustry maintains a physical sales force deployed across Europe visiting Fortune 500, OEMs, liquidators, and SMEs sourcing well-priced and quality equipment for upload to the website. In turn, ensuring that high volumes of good equipment are uploaded, attracts buyers who are drawn to deep choice of products and the hope of finding a good bargain.

This is just a small glimpse into the inner workings and market dynamics of a best-in-breed B2B start-up. In conclusion, of course, it remains to be seen how trading platforms such as GoIndustry will develop. However, with GoIndustry's compelling value proposition, aggressive execution, and full range of offline and online capabilities, the company is well on track to become the leading global asset recovery player in this market.

The e-roadmapping analysis

In light of the above and several interviews with GoIndustry's senior management, an e-roadmapping analysis has been conducted in order to determine the firm's positioning in the digital environment and its future development path. This section highlights issues that seem to be of particular importance in the context of the four axes of our strategy web, that is, customer centricity, value metrics, technology, and organisational configuration. In conclusion, the overall assessment of GoIndustry's digital strategy and operative execution in terms of the eRI will be presented. One has to bear in mind that the following represents an outsider's view at a distinct point of time and thus might gradually change over time.

With regard to the customer centricity axis, GoIndustry's strategy regarding customer intimacy, customer value, degree of segmentation, and branding has been examined. First, the firm's approach to generate customer intimacy and knowledge comprises key account management activities, the use of CRM and data mining tools, usability testing, and the constant monitoring of customer needs through sales force and call centre staff. This strategy aims at acquiring major supplier accounts, at streamlining the buyer segmentation, at retaining corporate customers, and at integrating customers into the development of new product and service offerings. Second, the customer value is inherently limited by GoIndustry's business focus on used or surplus equipment. Thus, the repeat offering and purchase susceptibility is relatively low in comparison to products that are exchanged between businesses on a regular basis. In order to overcome this problem and to leverage the customer lifetime value, GoIndustry has taken the opportunity to enhance and deepen their offering by integrating value-added services such as inspection of goods or asset valuation as well as the extension of the existing asset classes to replenishment and spare parts. Third, the segmentation and profiling processes of different account types on the supply and on the buy side are fairly sophisticated. In the future, one-to-one relationships can be initiated and supported by key account management and leveraged by technology. Finally, the brand value is seen as a sub-topic as its influence on buying decisions of corporate participants is relatively low. Nonetheless, brand value might be of considerable importance in competitive situations with online or offline rivals. Whereas GoIndustry has been able to position itself very successfully in industry publications and business rankings, the branding efforts can be intensified and the change of brand value over time, that is, the effectiveness and efficiency of branding activities, require active monitoring. The overall composition of the customer centricity system is well developed and particularly the depth of the various complementary elements from customer intimacy to segmentation can serve as a benchmark for the industry.

In terms of corporate governance, GoIndustry applies various value metrics such as acquisition and sourcing targets as well as revenue and profitability ratios. These metrics can be further refined, complemented, and finally integrated into an holistic strategic navigational model, that is, developing a cockpit view of corporate governance and performance monitoring. Regarding the market valuation, a real option perspective is used to determine the business model in terms of the upcoming endgame and the positioning in promising fields of activity. Major

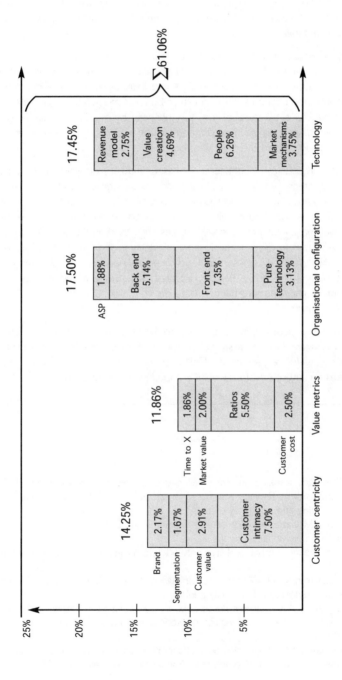

Figure 4.4.11 GoIndustry eRI score

milestones, in terms of speed in development and execution of GoIndustry's strategy, are time-to-technology development, time-to-second round of funding, and time-to-profitability.

GoIndustry's position on the technology axis is characterised by seamless online transaction processing including order entry, invoicing, and payment as well as an advanced integration of corporate suppliers and logistics service providers. As a means to diagonalise elements of GoIndustry's business model and to capitalise on existing competencies, this position can be enhanced by offering ASP services to corporate participants such as inventory compilation in order to increase lock-in of customers and to broaden the revenue model.

Regarding the organisational configuration axis, GoIndustry displays an impressive performance in areas such as channel portfolio, technological and industry know-how, expertise and mix of human resources as well as the scalability of the business model. The revenue model which is currently based on transaction fees can be complemented by further revenue sources such as shares from value-added services or ASP fees in order to achieve sustainability in the long term. Moreover, additional value-driving business segments need to be continuously identified, entered, and exploited. Thus, a flexible organisational structure and the ability to rapidly adopt to changing internal and external conditions are key to the future success of GoIndustry.

To conclude this e-roadmapping analysis Figure 4.4.11 displays GoIndustry's ratings within the four axes of our strategy web. While the firm is one of the most professional and successful players in the Digital Economy, the analysis reveals many opportunities for future development of competitive differentiation.

Notes

1. Bain & Company ranking in *Focus Money*: http://www.money.de/PM3D/PM3DB/PM3DBX/pm3dbx.htm. Ranking was based on an evaluation of business idea, management team, funding, and other key metrics
2. Blodget, Henry; McCabe, Edward: *The B2B Market Maker Book*, February 2000, USA, p. 5
3. Chart created on www.Ukinvest.com
4. Intranet is a company internal local area network which can usually be viewed with a web browser
5. Berlecon Research, Dr T. Wichmann: *B2B Marktplätze in Deutschland – Status quo, Chancen, Herausforderungen*, Berlin, July 2000
6. Figures quoted by A.T. Kearney: *Building the B2B Foundation – Positioning Net Market Makers for Success*, paper presenting research commissioned by Casbah Corporation, A.T. Kearney, 2000, p. 3
7. Calculations based on primary source data submitted as 10-K and 10-Q reports to the US Securities and Exchange Commission. Annual revenues refers to LTM (last twelve months)

8. Figures from CSFB, US Department of Commerce, Goldman Sachs
9. *Tradeout*, 1999
10. Advertising Association of the UK, 1997
11. Credit Suisse First Boston Technology Group: *B2B Evolution – Providing the Missing Link in the Supply/Demand Chain*, CSFB Corporation, May 2000
12. CSFB Technology Group Analysis, US Department of Commerce raw data
13. A.T. Kearney: *Building the B2B Foundation – Positioning Net Market Makers for Success*, paper presenting research commissioned by Casbah Corporation, A.T. Kearney, 2000, p. 2

DaimlerChrysler Five Star Market Center: A Roadmap for Small Business e-procurement

Market Center Development Team, eConnect Platform, DaimlerChrysler

CHAPTER CONTENTS

Introduction

The Five Star Market Center was conceived and founded by a team in the Retail Strategies group of DaimlerChrysler's US headquarters in Auburn Hills, Michigan responsible for US Chrysler, Dodge and Jeep franchises ('dealers'). The team recognised two competitive forces that potentially threaten the future of the traditional independent franchised auto dealer: first, increased worldwide production capacity that exceeds forecast demand by nearly 50 per cent in the foreseeable future; second, the potential for Internet-based e-commerce to dramatically shift methods of sales and service for automotive products and affiliated services. Both issues impact the future success of both the corporation and its dealers, with any potential solution providing a clear two-way benefit.

On record as the company that has stood and will continue to stand firmly behind and fully support its dealers during this period of transition, the team developed several initiatives aimed to decrease the cost of distribution as the retail strategy for facing the increasingly competitive market. The Five Star

Market Center (FSMC) is one of those initiatives, aimed specifically at dealers, with the goal of reducing dealers' indirect overhead expenditure.

The FSMC was made public in a press release dated 20 September 1999, at which time it was described as the corporation's first e-commerce B2B initiative using the Internet for dealers, connecting them with corporate suppliers to provide purchasing price advantages at corporate-volume discounts previously not available to dealers.

Since then both FSMC and the corporation's e-commerce initiatives have matured greatly, with FSMC being a part of the eConnect Platform Team, a US operating group of DaimlerChrysler's DCXNet business unit, aimed at making DaimlerChrysler an 'e' company.

This contribution depicts the development path from concept in September 1999 through pilot launch in January 2000 and rollout to all 4400 US Chrysler, Dodge and Jeep dealers in August 2000. Rollout is not to be confused with completion of the initiative, which is frankly in its mere infancy of operation and potential benefit to the dealers. What follows are descriptions of the business model, the launch 'realities', the organisation, and what are believed to be the long-term sustainable advantages.

Business model

The value proposition at concept

Figure 4.5.1 demonstrates the fundamental vision of the FSMC, an inter-mediary between the corporation's strategic suppliers and the dealer network. The initial goal of the Five Star Market Center was:

> to leverage the value of DaimlerChrysler's Extended Enterprise of Suppliers to reduce dealers' cost of purchasing indirect goods and services and to improve the efficiencies of that process using Internet technology.

FSMC provides an Internet link from its 4400 Chrysler, Dodge and Jeep dealers, to its numerous strategic suppliers of indirect goods and services products. Participation in the FSMC is voluntary for both dealers and suppliers, with value the motivator that drives participation. The 'market center' is private primarily to ensure that supplier 'deals' are not extended beyond the intended dealer audience, as well as containing participation to Chrysler, Dodge and Jeep dealers for strategic advantage of the corporation.

Importantly and unlike most other 'exchanges', the FSMC role ends at the point of linking agent, with commerce taking place through direct

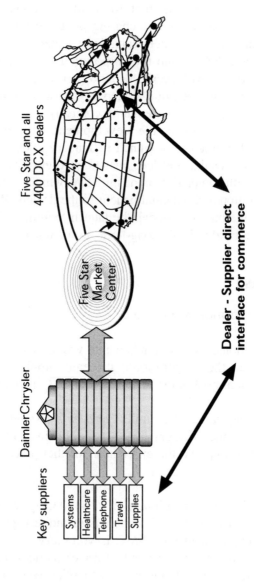

FIVE STAR
MARKETCENTER   Value proposition – concept

DaimlerChrysler

Key suppliers

Five Star and all
4400 DCX dealers

Five Star
Market
Center

Systems
Healthcare
Telephone
Travel
Supplies

**Dealer - Supplier direct
interface for commerce**

Figure 4.5.1   Market Center vision

dealer–supplier interface. This yields an infrastructure cost efficiency which drives further savings into the dealer and supplier.

Value for the participating dealer is derived from the implicit assumption that dealers would find lower prices in the FSMC than they generally negotiate on their own, due to the corporation's contracts with suppliers that contain negotiated prices based upon the corporation's volume purchasing discounts.

Value for the participating supplier is motivated by potential sales to an expanded market for their products and services at minimal cost of marketing. 'Factory endorsement' is assumed to deliver the marketing required for dealer participation in many cases.

The value to DaimlerChrysler extends beyond the intrinsic dealer benefit to the potential to drive further volume discounts through aggregation of corporate and dealer purchases. In fact, the aggregate dealer financial statement summaries unveiled the 4400 dealers in total purchase approximately the same amount as the corporation in the US market, each about US$3.5 billion. There are many commodities where the dealers purchase more than the corporation.

The original FSMC launch plan consisted of developing an Internet website that simply linked dealers to corporate suppliers' websites. It required dealers to '*do the shopping' for themselves* among those suppliers to evaluate if there are any goods and/or services that fulfil their needs at an advantageous price versus that achieved on their own.

The Indianapolis pilot, beginning in January 2000 with nine dealers and a single supplier (office supplies), demonstrated that while the business model was feasible, many differences between the dealer purchasing process and the corporate purchasing process would make the 'simple link' between dealers and suppliers insufficient to provide long-term value-add.

That came primarily from what we learned about the dealer purchasing process:

■ There are as many processes as there are dealers, if not more

■ Many people are buyers at dealerships, most commonly tied to a dealership's five core departments: New Vehicle Sales, Used Vehicle Sales, Service, Parts, and Finance

■ Those buyers often purchase the same commodity from different suppliers without knowing so

■ Or if they have established a preferred supplier, the buyers sometimes purchase the same item the same day or only days apart without knowing so

- The purchasing process has not been carefully constructed or managed at most dealerships

- Information on dealership purchases is not well measured in most cases, and is rarely studied.

This learning impacted the FSMC business model from that of a linking intermediary to that of a strategic value-added process intermediary. The simple link placed too much burden on the dealership user to 'do the shopping' to make the model work in the long term. While dealer buyers know their needs at any given time, we found them to be different to corporate needs in many cases.

That is, corporate goods and services are negotiated and suppliers selected based on a carefully constructed request for quote (RFQ) with detailed specifications based upon the corporation's needs and desire for consistency on an ongoing basis. Not so for dealers, leaving many instances where the corporate specifications do not meet the needs of the dealers. Goods and services for a corporation may be 'over-spec'd' or 'under-spec'd' for any given buyer at a dealership, for a dealership overall, or for dealers in aggregate. The result is conflict of product, price or customer service if simple transfer is attempted.

The Indianapolis pilot demonstrated that a change was required to the initial model to ensure long-term success. The FSMC team concluded that a model that depends on many dealership 'buyers' to go out of their way to do their own shopping, using a new tool as difficult and slow as the Internet tends to be, within a procurement environment as chaotic and disorganised as what we found among the dealers, did not deliver on the promise of price advantages or process efficiencies required to truly lower the dealers' costs.

There was too much risk of success depending on process change on behalf of the dealers and associated investment in time and resources on the part of the suppliers to move forward in this manner, especially being the corporation's first significant e-commerce B2B initiative.

The value proposition in reality – three-way partnership

The revised 'real world partnership' value proposition is shown in Figure 4.5.2.

Key differences include two-way dealership links, direct supplier links and the corporate dependency decreased to an indirect relationship with the procurement and supply group as relates to the strategic suppliers.

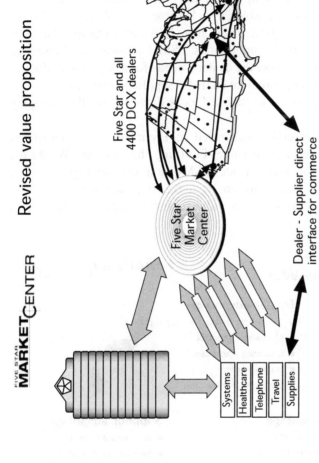

Revised value proposition

Figure 4.5.2 Revised value proposition

The revised FSMC is more customer-driven, more strategic, yet far more burdened with direct responsibility for managing the dealer–supplier linkage and the associated value derivation. Unfortunately, it is also slower to implement. The critical difference shifts the burden of shopping from the dealers to FSMC.

The burden of shopping requires the FSMC to make *specification* a core competency, including product, price and customer service.

What was conceived as simple voluntary links between dealers and suppliers with FSMC as an enabler, now became carefully managed links to a controlled group of suppliers who have best met RFQ specifications for a commodity or group of commodities. FSMC negotiates and endorses the single best supplier to meet the dealers' needs for any given product or service, providing current corporate strategic suppliers' first priority.

Indeed, FSMC's promise to the dealers is now 'We do the shopping for you'.

The three-way partnership described in Figure 4.5.3 demonstrates FSMC's role in delivering real value. Fulfilling the promise 'We do the shopping for you' to the dealers places FSMC in a more strategic position, a truly private marketplace driven by a specific customer that seeks enterprise-wide cost savings and value enhancement as a long-term strategic advantage.

The Win–Win–Win

FIVE STAR
MARKETCENTER

Dealer advantage
- Lower cost through leveraged pricing
- Management control
- Operating efficiencies
- Support services
- e-commerce innovation

Chrysler Group advantage
- Five Star advantage/dealer loyalty
- Increased volume, purchasing leverage
- Transaction fees cover costs
- Real-time market data
- e-commerce innovation

Supplier advantage
- Increased volume, sales
- Reduced 'cost of sales'
- Aggregated demand
- Expanded market data
- e-commerce innovation

Figure 4.5.3   The partnership business model

Whereas the initial concept simply leveraged existing supplier contracts to drive savings for dealers, the partnership business model begins with the customer requirement, develops the enterprise-wide means of meeting that requirement at lowest cost, and strives to implement the solution.

Organisation and core competencies

Figure 4.5.4 shows the seven core competencies that drive the FSMC operations. Each is described in summary below:

1. *Customer knowledge* is the first value-added competency. This knowledge includes several aspects of the procurement equation:

   - What do dealers purchase?
   - How much of any given item do dealers purchase and what is the price?
   - What is the process they use to purchase and secure it currently?

   We develop this knowledge primarily through surveys among a group of dealers who have agreed to work with the team during the Market Center development. This knowledge drives straight into commodity specification.

2. *Commodity specification* includes not only the product, but also the required price and customer service for any given supplier to fulfil dealer needs. Taken together, the 'specs' assist commodity target prioritisation, based on size of overall dealer spending and potential savings based on the new FSMC operating model. Specification is also used to determine whether the Internet-based ordering by dealers is by cata-

Five Star Market Center

- Customer knowledge
- Commodity specification
- Supplier selection
- Supplier management
- Marketing/Customer service
- Billing and payment
- Reporting

Figure 4.5.4 Core competencies

logue, subscription, or a new value-added process. This specification also includes a FSMC cost vs. dealer price, enabling FSMC to earn transaction fees (see point 6 below for more details).

3. *Supplier selection* is accomplished much as any other would be driven by the specification, with two exceptions: first, priority is given to current DCX suppliers to maximise the potential future aggregation of corporate and dealer purchase volumes although this is not a requirement, and second, based upon the supplier's willingness to drive their business to the Internet.

4. *Supplier enablement and management* is the value-added design phase of FSMC. This collaborative design effort leverages FSMC knowledge of dealership operations and suppliers' commodity expertise. The combined enablement team works together to develop a new, more cost-efficient process of meeting dealer needs for any given commodity. A simple example is overnight 'airmail', which FSMC learned is 85 per cent within 100 miles of a dealership – meaning delivery via ground service could be substituted at significant cost savings.

5. *Marketing and customer service* are the first obvious value advantages provided by participating suppliers, whereby FSMC leverages the DCX corporate means of communicating with its dealers – a significant endorsement the dealers watch closely. Regarding customer service, FSMC has established a dedicated customer service centre as the 'single point of contact' for dealer resolution when any issue occurs. In some cases, the dealer will be forwarded to the supplier from the FSMC customer service centre if that is deemed the appropriate response to drive issue resolution.

6. *Consolidated billing and payment* is the one means by which FSMC gains visibility to the dealer–supplier transactions, albeit after the fact. This is a function that drives significant cost and process efficiency for both dealers and suppliers. FSMC leverages DCX back-end systems to accomplish both dealer billing and supplier payment. There are three primary functions here:

   ▪ Suppliers submit a consolidated bill to FSMC for all dealer purchases
   ▪ FSMC deconsolidates each bill and invoices the appropriate dealers
   ▪ FSMC pays the suppliers on behalf of the dealers.

   FSMC delivers significant cost savings for suppliers by eliminating the need to individually invoice 4400 dealers and by assuming the dealer credit risk. These 'efficiency savings' are invested back to deliver an advantage in FSMC dealer pricing.

Consolidated billing also delivers cost savings and process enhancement for dealers, by collecting their purchasing activity into one account. This same account is also used for many goods and service purchases made by dealers from DCX, such as service parts and training. This account will increasingly deliver procurement information dealers have not previously had available, providing enhanced accounting control and process opportunities.

Fulfilling the billing function enables FSMC to earn a modest 'billing and administration fee', the sole means of revenue generation. The fee is accomplished by negotiating two prices with the suppliers for virtually every item available on the FSMC: FSMC cost and dealer price. The differential between cost and price is the revenue earned.

This two-price scenario is somewhat unique versus the more-typical mark-up price model, however, price transparency is reflective of the supplier partnership.

Importantly, the two-price model is a requirement given the 'link-out' website technology utilised, whereby the dealers conduct business on the suppliers' websites. That is, suppliers must display the marked-up price (dealer price) on their websites for the dealer to see the correct price, and to enable the suppliers to collect all applicable sales taxes for dealer purchases. This model has the secondary benefit of relieving FSMC from the liability of ownership of the goods and services sold, eliminating tax burden and any potential product/service liability.

7. *Reporting* is the glue that keeps the parties in the game, including dealer usage and savings, supplier website activity and billings, and FSMC throughput and revenue. It is also the means for developing the dynamics to ensure FSMC and its suppliers remain viable and valid to the dealers over time. The model provides tremendous opportunities to leverage data assets. FSMC intends to provide its strategic partners with valuable information concerning demand, shifts in demand, pricing, customer service, and so on.

These seven core competencies account for the primary functioning of the FSMC on a day-to-day basis. Given the initiative is in its infancy, the seven functions are primarily accomplished the 'old fashioned way' – with people interacting to accomplish detailed action plans. Over time it is believed that some of those functions will be able to be systematised electronically, but those that truly add value will likely continue to require collaboration among smart people.

Market and competition

It is surprising to realise that with all the activity going on in e-commerce regarding e-procurement, auto dealers have been only minimally targeted to date, although they represent by far the largest retail business in aggregate in the country. Perhaps that is due to the complexities of the business, as the FSMC team learned early on with the Indianapolis pilot, or perhaps it is due to the close relationship between the manufacturers and the dealerships.

The 'bullseye' proximity diagram shown in Figure 4.5.5 is how the FSMC team views the competition. With the dealers as the target in the middle, the concentric rings around them represent potential competitors and the degree to which differing groups have share-of-mind or potential best-penetration opportunity for e-procurement solutions.

Starting from the outermost ring, FSMC has experienced very few dealers using public e-procurement solutions in their businesses at this time, such as Priceline.com. There is somewhat more usage of the specialised solutions that address one department of their business, such as

Figure 4.5.5   Auto dealer e-procurement options

Grainger.com and ToolSource.com for tools for the service and parts departments, but even that remains limited at this time.

Interestingly, the auto dealer-specific start-ups have also done poorly to date, with dealers indicating that none of them provides the convenience and real value they promise. Our jury evaluation demonstrated that while these solutions recognise the idiosyncrasies of the auto dealership users, there is too much added complexity for the users to take advantage of the new tool, even as a short-term experiment. Each of these has resorted to an added function, such as training, to drive itself into the dealership environment.

As far as FSMC is aware, no other manufacturers currently offer a competitive solution to the FSMC described here, or plan to in the foreseeable future. We have found a number of specific 'deals' that manufacturers have cut with select suppliers to provide services to dealers, but none that demonstrates a strategy, or that delivers enterprise value like that of FSMC.

The most potent competition is the one closest to the current dealership software users, that is the dealership systems provider (DSP), such as ADP. Virtually every dealership uses a DSP system for supporting primary functions such as human resources and accounting at a minimum. Many people around the dealerships interface with these systems, so they have a built-in user group. While the DSPs are only experimenting with e-procurement at this point, their dealership-specific systems expertise and overall dealer knowledge yield a significant advantage in their ability to penetrate e-procurement activity should they target it. Indeed, DSPs appear to be the primary competitor to FSMC now and in the future.

The issue for success among the DSPs will be timing. Today's DSP environments are primarily client–server architecture (75+ per cent), a roadblock to widespread DSP penetration into e-procurement in the near term. The indication is that major DSPs plan to shift to web-based architecture over the coming two or three years, which only makes sense for the dealership systems environment as a whole, given the manufacturers' indications of intent to shift their future communications with the dealers to web-based architecture. We expect the DSPs to seek e-procurement partnerships in the near term as a defensive offering for dealers who indicate a desire to shift their purchasing operations in a new direction.

Over time we expect the DSP–e-procurement partnerships to deliver dealer-specific commodities and processes, which will be strong competition depending on the value equation.

Structural competitive advantage

The Five Star Market Center has three key characteristics that provide it with a long-term structural advantage:

- Aggregating dealer demand
- Leveraging existing manufacturer strategic suppliers
- Protecting supplier margins.

These are demonstrated in the analysis shown in Table 4.5.1, which provides a comparison of the four e-procurement providers described in the section on 'market and competition' above against the key criteria determined to be required for near-term dealership adaptation and long-term integration.

It is the FSMC team's evaluation that no other competitor can accomplish aggregating demand for best price while leveraging current supplier relations and protecting supplier margins, particularly in combination.

Bottom line it means FSMC's ultimate structural advantage is its unique relationship with its DCX manufacturer parent, which delivers a combination of existing dealer relations and supplier relations. The FSMC model repurposes those relations to build a new business, a business that is advantageous to both the dealers and the customers.

The FSMC team believes it is very telling that the long-term structural advantage of its model has nothing to do with technology at all. Technology is certainly an important element, the enabler to building a new business in an expedient and cost-efficient manner. But at the end of the day, success appears to be entirely dependent upon relationships, bringing people together in a new way.

Table 4.5.1   Competitive structural analysis: ability to meet dealership e-procurement requirements

	FSMC	DSP	Dealer	Public
Customer knowledge	+	+	+	−
Aggregate demand for best price	+	0	0	−
Scope of product/service	+	+	+	−
Dealer process efficiency	+	+	+	0
Integrate with dealer systems	+	++	0	0
Leverage supplier relations	++	0	0	0
Protect supplier margins	+	0	0	−
Total '+'	8	5	3	0

The e-roadmapping analysis

The subsequent e-roadmapping analysis will focus on FSMC's core competencies in relation to our *organisational configuration* axis. The depth of these seven competencies further illuminates that the viability of such a service offering can only be generated through the agglomeration of a deep industry and process know-how. The analysis will emphasise that it is this expertise that enabled DCX to engage in such a concrete form of a *diagonalisation* strategy. The analysis is completed with some recommendations that seem to be promising opportunities for leveraging FSMC's capabilities and existing relationships.

As was mentioned earlier, the FSMC's business model is shaped by the following seven core competencies: customer knowledge, commodity specification, supplier selection, supplier management, marketing and customer service, billing and payment, and reporting. Thus we will now take a look at the details of these competencies in contrast to the possible concretisations as specified in our eRI.

First, *customer knowledge* is generated through surveys among a selected group of dealers. Thus, potential participants of the platform have been integrated in the solution development process at an early stage. This customer knowledge might be continuously updated and refined through focus group studies and/or Internet-based surveys. The systemic use of customer information can enhance customer retention, accelerate the adoption among potential participants, increase transaction volumes, and constitutes a sustainable competitive advantage. This extensive information about dealers' preferences and distinct needs drives the second core competence, that is *commodity specification*, regarding products, prices, and service offerings. Moreover, by selecting and qualifying current DCX suppliers to participate in the FSMC, value is being generated to the advantage of suppliers, dealers, and the parent company DCX. Therefore, the third competence constitutes a threefold leverage of existing *supplier relationships*. The value creation dimension is being reinforced by the fourth core ability to manage the collaborative commerce position, that is, to capitalise on FSMC's industry know-how and the suppliers' commodity experience. As a result, the enabling and *management of suppliers* leads to cost-efficient exchange processes between suppliers and dealers. FSMC's *marketing and customer service* centre as a single point of contact for connected dealers leverages existing means of communication between DCX and the dealer network. Hence, first-level support is provided by a central, highly specialised unit which should, on the one hand, reduce administration and overhead costs on the suppliers' side, and, on the other hand, ensure an adequate service level on the customers' side. Moreover, FSMC can enhance its understanding of customer needs and deepen the relationship to its connected participants. The sixth core competence – consolidated *billing and payment* – capitalises on existing back-end invoicing and payment systems of the parent company DCX and constitutes a value-added service offering, which leads to cost savings for suppliers and dealers, which generates procurement and transactions data, and which is the foundation of the FSMC's revenue model. The information generation is complemented by the *reporting* ability which provides tremendous opportunities to leverage data assets and to offer business intelligence services.

To put it in a nutshell, the FSMC initiative is an illustrative example for the above-mentioned *diagonalisation* strategy as it takes DaimlerChrysler's established relationships to suppliers and dealers, existing IT applications, and in-depth industry know-how as the starting point to leverage these assets to the advantage of dealers, suppliers, and the parent company itself and offers an innovative service to corporate dealers.

In light of the above, the following recommendations for future strategic moves of FSMC can be deduced: first, the firm's value-added services offering could be complemented in breadth through, for example, logistics services and/or in depth through, for example, financing or leasing offerings. Thus, the FSMC initiative would anticipate a general trend in business-to-business commerce towards *one-stop solutions* for corporate customers. Moreover, additional value-added services might constitute a further revenue source and hence broaden the profit model of FSMC. Second, the company's current value proposition could be offered to additional third parties such as big DCX clients like car rental firms or public transport providers or even to completely non-related companies. This would again increase cost advantages for all parties, drive revenue growth of FSMC, and generate additional amounts of procurement spend and also transaction data.

Siemens: The Transformation into an Application Service Provider

Stefan Holler, Vice-President, Siemens Business Services, Management Consulting

CHAPTER CONTENTS

The purpose of this case study is to delineate the reasoning for Siemens I&C (information and communication) to enter the ASP market. To be able to do so meaningfully, it is important to show the overall organisational configuration of Siemens detailing all available skills and competencies. Furthermore the sub-chapter provides an in-depth review of developments in the worldwide ASP market and is closed out by depicting the current Siemens ASP offering.

Anatomy of Siemens I&C for ASP providing

Successful operation as an ASP depends on a formidable mix of qualities. The business must have the contract management and application support skills of an IT provider, the network and data management expertise of a full enterprise ISP, and the online instincts of a portal operator. All of these capabilities can be found within Siemens I&C.

Siemens I&C is one of the global players for communication systems and networks as well as for IT networks.

The joint venture Fujitsu Siemens Computers became the new number one European IT company practically overnight, and it aims to capture a leading global position in markets for personal computers, Intel based and UNIX servers, and large-scale enterprise systems.

Fujitsu Siemens, the leading European computer company, has announced 'ASPect' – a major new initiative aimed at establishing the company as the number one supplier of server technology for the emerging European ASP Application Service Provider and Application Hosting market.

The company is targeting ASP-related revenues of EUR 250 million by 2003, and expects the ASP sector to become a key market for its leading-edge Intel and SPARC-based server systems. As part of the ASPect initiative Fujitsu Siemens Computers (FSC) has launched the first European ASP Centre which will be based in Munich and will be operational in Q1, 2000.

FSC expects the demand in Europe for ASP solutions to grow significantly during the next two years – not just at the high end but increasingly for the growing number of small and medium-size companies attracted by a lower overall cost of ownership of ASP solutions. Major target is to support independent software vendors (ISVs) to web-enable their solutions for customers in the small and medium-size market. Web-enabled vertical solutions shall be available on FSC Intel and SPARC-based server platforms.

The company's new ASP Competence Centre features a fully-equipped data centre backed by a comprehensive communications and IT infrastructure. In addition to switches, routers, firewalls, and high-speed two MByte/sec Internet access, the company is working with major telco carriers and providers to integrate the ASP centre into a European Internet backbone.

Access to the ASP Centre is also available by ISDN connection. The new Fujitsu Siemens Computers ASP Centre will support Windows NT, Linux and Solaris applications, initially running on 12 servers including PRIMERGY Intel-based systems and the new SPARC-based GP7000F Solaris system. With its dynamically re-configurable partitioning capability the new GP7000F is particularly suitable for major ASP implementations.

The Fujitsu Siemens Computers ASP Centre will serve as a resource for ISVs looking to web-enable their applications, and will also offer benchmarking, sizing, and a testing environment for ISVs. The company will also provide certification of both general and project-specific ASP solutions.

Fujitsu Siemens Computers is an executive member of the ASP Industry Consortium, the international group formed to promote the Application Service Provider industry by sponsoring research, fostering standards, and articulating the measurable benefits of the evolving ASP delivery model. ASP Centre staff is backed by the company's extensive network of several thousand support specialists.

Siemens Business Services (SBS) has the span of expertise to find the best way to synchronise business processes and technology opportunities in more than 40 countries and offers the full service range from professional services and consulting to operations.

To reinforce the excellent market position of Siemens I&C, over US$2.2 billion have been invested in research and development in the

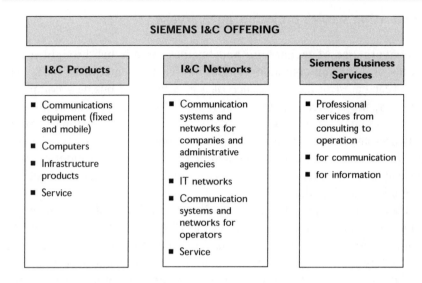

Figure 4.6.1   Siemens I&C content

fiscal year 1999. In the process, four strategic fields have been defined. These fields are devices, IP-based networks, wireless networks, and business solutions. The comprehensive know-how in each of these areas is unique and not normally found within a single company. In this context, Siemens I&C is one source for the most complex convergence solutions (Figure 4.6.1).

Beyond the pureplay ASPs, the players in the ASP arena will emerge from three general areas (or a combination thereof):

- Professional service companies
- Infrastructure vendors
- Independent software vendors (ISVs).

Siemens I&C is heavily represented in all these areas and offers nearly all products and services which are needed in the ASP value chain.

ASP is a very important subject within Siemens I&C. The particular positioning of Siemens I&C in the ASP market by using experience, know-how, and resources but also by transforming existing capabilities into the e-business and New Economy world is shown later in this chapter.

Application service provision: an overview

A convergence of technology and business trends has brought a new means of acquiring computing within the reach of enterprises today. The past year has seen the emergence of a new breed of business computing provider, the application service provider. This next generation information technology services company delivers computing to customers from a network-based data centre. Enterprises no longer have to own or operate the hardware and software on which their business computing runs. Instead they pay a fee to the ASP according to various pricing models, for example usage based.

The concept of hosted applications is not new. It probably had its beginnings in the mainframe timeshares of the 1960s and 70s. In 1962 the EDS company founded by Ross Perot had the idea to put resources for data processing at the disposal of companies which did not have their own resources or knowledge or did not see data processing as a core competence which should be kept inside.

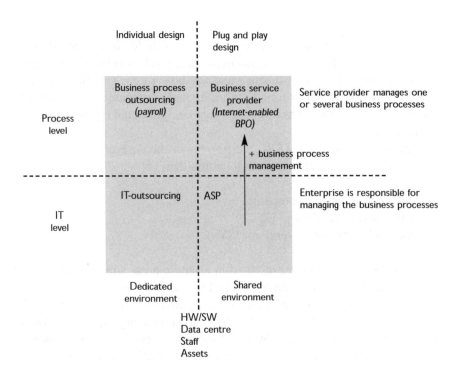

Figure 4.6.2   Domains of enterprise application outsourcing

The IT-outsourcing was born. The concept of outsourcing is increasingly accepted in business today. Management gurus and investors alike emphasise the merits of concentrating on core competence, and on bringing in outside specialists to perform all non-essential functions.

Generally, four domains of enterprise application outsourcing exist which differentiate by process, IT, and environment handling (Figure 4.6.2).

By development of the Internet technology, website hosting became a very popular outsourcing service. Providers have developed special offerings which were tailored to the demands of either small, medium or large companies. It is not known when the first Internet-based corporate application was outsourced. But software rental by Internet is already a common practice in the US and will be more emphasised in Europe in the future.

In May 1999, a group of 25 companies in the US founded the *application service provider consortium* which has now more than 100 members. Major target of the consortium is to foster the ASP branch by supporting research, by defining standards, and by making the advantages of the ASP model public.

Currently, there is competition between more than 100 application service providers worldwide. These providers differentiate by the offered applications and by scope of technical and IT services.

The ASP industry consortium defines an ASP as:

essentially, a supplier who makes applications available on a subscription basis. An ASP is a business partner that provides choices regarding how software applications are managed and delivered.

The Gartner Group sees an ASP as follows:

ASPs deliver application functionality and associated services across a network to multiple customers using a rental pricing model.

Even if application service provision is a variation of outsourcing, it is very important to understand that ASP business is different to what is widely understood as 'traditional outsourcing business'. Outsourcing is very often a highly customised application for a *1:1 relationship* with heavy focus on large companies. The ASP business mainly uses standard products focused on all customer groups by having a *one-to-many relationship*. There are major differences in terms of characteristics, target customers, and value proposition (Figure 4.6.3).

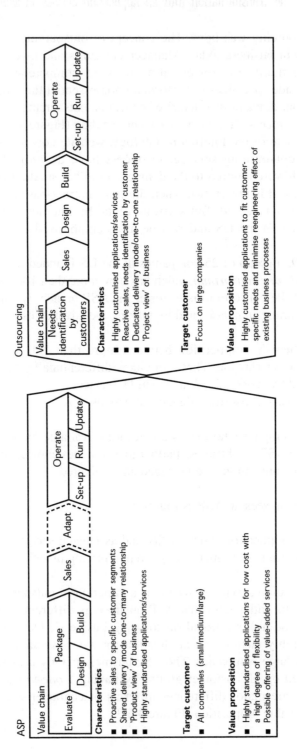

Figure 4.6.3 Contrasting ASP and outsourcing

The online ASP idea as a viable option in mainstream enterprise computing is fostered by the upcoming market and technology trends.

Market

■ *Tendency to outsourcing*
Many businesses now outsource specific elements of their total IT infrastructure to an outside service provider, including the network operation and provision, the monitoring of service levels, and increasingly the provision of specific applications themselves.

The spectrum of application services now available as a managed service ranges from simple website design packages, passing through hosted e-mail and messaging, right up to high-end enterprise resource planning (ERP) applications.

■ *A wired economy*
Businesses today have accepted the need to get wired. The prevalence of e-commerce and e-business is spreading over the whole world. As a result, today many aspects of enterprise computing are moving into an Internet-centric model (Figure 4.6.4).

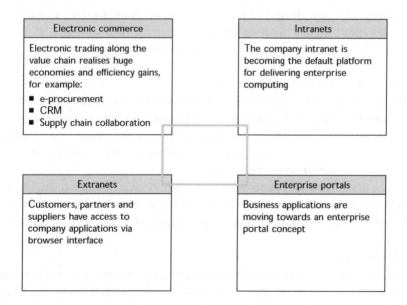

Electronic commerce	Intranets
Electronic trading along the value chain realises huge economies and efficiency gains, for example: ■ e-procurement ■ CRM ■ Supply chain collaboration	The company intranet is becoming the default platform for delivering enterprise computing

Extranets	Enterprise portals
Customers, partners and suppliers have access to company applications via browser interface	Business applications are moving towards an enterprise portal concept

Figure 4.6.4   Enterprise computing in the Internet age

Many businesses rely on outside providers to operate the infrastructure for these new computing architectures. These outside providers are often better equipped than their customers to handle the delivery of applications across a wide area network.

Technology

Various emerging technologies over the past two to three years have combined to make application services a cost-effective and accessible option today.

▪ *Universal IP networking*
The Internet's underlying Internet protocol (IP) is becoming the default standard architecture for all forms of telecommunications. The advent of the Internet has demonstrated the viability of a simple, open, platform-independent network protocol that delivers both content and applications to users cheaply and easily.

▪ *Server-based computing*
Cheaper, more plentiful telecommunications have in turn encouraged the development of server-based computing architectures. These server architectures are designed for environments where client computers access centralised servers on which most of the data storage and application processing take place across a telecommunication link.

▪ *Distributed systems' management*
Easier connectivity has revolutionised systems' management enabling computer systems to be monitored, managed, and even repaired across a phone line. This has been a major contributor to the emergence of selective outsourcing enabling reliable remote management from a centralised enterprise operations centre.
These market and technology trends have been combined to enable the application service providers we see coming to market today. They offer a broad ASP spectrum of solutions, operating models and delivery choices.

▪ *Web-top applications*
Examples include e-mail and collaborative applications, file or document storage, web and e-commerce site builders, simple desktop productivity tools and so on. These applications have been developed from ground up as Internet offerings and are provided either free or at a very low

subscription cost. Additionally, software-based online business services are very important. By using the Internet, multiple services from e-purchasing to specialist professional services are offered in a cost-effective way. Currently there are very few examples of core enterprise applications being offered in this model. This is because established software products have to be reengineered for Internet delivery.

■ *Subscription outsourcing*
The model of high-end application services takes existing enterprise software products and offers them as outsourced applications on a subscription basis. The ASP tailors an application to the customer's requirement and purchases the necessary software and hardware. The customer receives the application as a managed service. In this way established enterprise applications like SAP, Siebel, and so on can be offered for a fixed per-user, per-month subscription payment across the life of the contract avoiding the high up-front commitment required for a conventional purchase (Figure 4.6.5).

■ *Application server hosting*
As websites have become more and more sophisticated, what started out as the provision of web and mail servers to business customers has

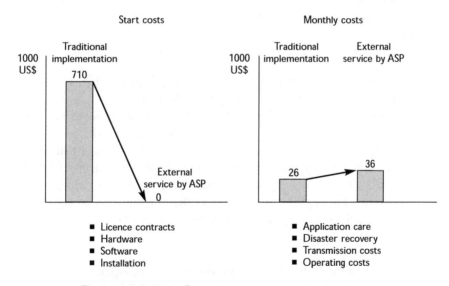

Figure 4.6.5   Comparing cost: traditional vs. ASP enterprise computing

ended up in a highly sophisticated managed infrastructure offering. In the process, web hosting providers have turned into application service providers. In the enterprise market, hosting providers have been drawn into providing increasingly complex intranet, extranet, and Internet services for their customers, often taking care of the provision, implementation and management of the server rather than simply providing data centre space.

A number of ASPs have extended the principle to other networked applications such as exchange and Notes e-mail and messaging systems. Today such providers are responsible for complex, mission-critical e-commerce and e-business applications on behalf of their customers.

Other providers have preferred to evolve their web hosting services to concentrate on managing server farms for dot-com enterprises and other application service providers turning into ASP infrastructure providers (AIPs).

ASP aggregators

As more and more applications become available as online services, a new type of ASP is beginning to emerge; one that integrates multiple applications into a coherent, aggregated offering. High-end ASPs are starting to build up portfolios of complementary enterprise applications, while at the entry level, online portals are gathering together collections of applications and business services to meet a particular need. Even some banks and telecom companies are becoming ASP aggregators to offer services to their small business customers.

Generally ASP providers can be found in four categories:

- *Internal IT departments* which provide company-wide applications and services for all departments and subsidiaries.

  Very often, internal IT departments have similar offers to an external ASP. They differentiate by payment of applications which means that corporate IT departments including hardware, software, and services are fully paid by the company. ASPs charge on a user-based price model or on a leasing basis. Furthermore, by using corporate IT services, the applications belong to the company, by using external ASP services, the applications belong to the ASP provider.

- *Pure ASPs*
  Pure application service providers are companies which see providing, caring and managing of software applications as their core

business. These are companies like Corio, Future Link, US Sinter-work, and so on.

- *Internet service providers (ISP)*
  Currently, more than 5000 Internet service providers exist worldwide. ISPs suffer from continuously falling prices for low value activities such as pure transmission capacity providing. Some of these companies see the ASP model as a possibility to enlarge their service offering and to compensate losses, but also to improve the retention of existing customers.

  Some examples are MCI Worldcom, PSI-Net, and GTE Internet-working. These well established companies with a broad range of services and transmission capacities are currently working on partnerships and co-operations with major software vendors such as SAP, PeopleSoft, Oracle, and so on. This should create a win–win situation for both ISPs and software vendors by keeping existing clients and reaching new customer groups.

- *Telcos as ASPs*
  They offer outsourced services as traditional telcos and cable TV providers aggressively try to enter the ASP market. They see the possibility to offer value-added services, for example e-mail applications, voice-over IP or workgroup application to keep and to enlarge their customer bases and make the business more profitable. Major examples are AT&T, Cable & Wireless, Qwest, BT, and Deutsche Telekom.

Additionally, hardware, software and component providers focus on ASP business to enhance their revenues by taking several parts in the ASP value chain as well as by co-operation with front-end ASP providers (Figure 4.6.6).

The value proposition of ASP services is to: enable customers to get accelerated and lower cost access to mission-critical applications; reduce capital investments; reduce total cost of ownership (30–50 per cent), simplify accounting; use best-practice (industry) process templates and use '80–20' IT solutions rather than over-engineering 'total' solutions. This results in more speed, focus and scalability, increased flexibility and reduced costs.

Application hosting is expected to place small and midsize companies on a level playing field with larger corporations without having to make

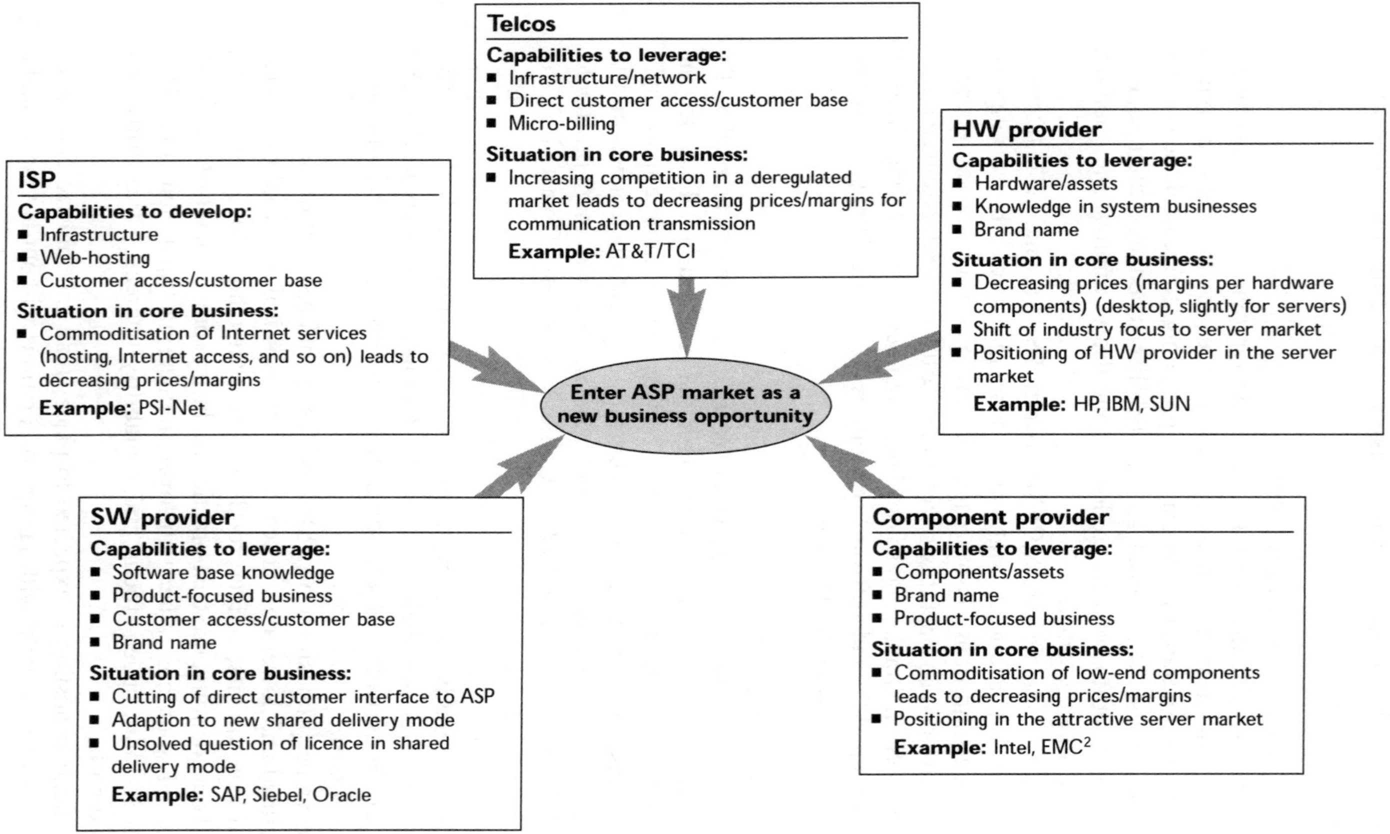

ISP

Capabilities to develop:
- Infrastructure
- Web-hosting
- Customer access/customer base

Situation in core business:
- Commoditisation of Internet services (hosting, Internet access, and so on) leads to decreasing prices/margins

Example: PSI-Net

Telcos

Capabilities to leverage:
- Infrastructure/network
- Direct customer access/customer base
- Micro-billing

Situation in core business:
- Increasing competition in a deregulated market leads to decreasing prices/margins for communication transmission

Example: AT&T/TCI

HW provider

Capabilities to leverage:
- Hardware/assets
- Knowledge in system businesses
- Brand name

Situation in core business:
- Decreasing prices (margins per hardware components) (desktop, slightly for servers)
- Shift of industry focus to server market
- Positioning of HW provider in the server market

Example: HP, IBM, SUN

Component provider

Capabilities to leverage:
- Components/assets
- Brand name
- Product-focused business

Situation in core business:
- Commoditisation of low-end components leads to decreasing prices/margins
- Positioning in the attractive server market

Example: Intel, EMC^2

SW provider

Capabilities to leverage:
- Software base knowledge
- Product-focused business
- Customer access/customer base
- Brand name

Situation in core business:
- Cutting of direct customer interface to ASP
- Adaption to new shared delivery mode
- Unsolved question of licence in shared delivery mode

Example: SAP, Siebel, Oracle

Enter ASP market as a new business opportunity

Figure 4.6.6 Potential ASP players

heavy investments in the IT personnel and infrastructure, necessary to support enterprise applications.

Hosted applications separate the server from the clients. The server becomes a property of the application service provider, not the customer. The customer pays for the use of the application in the same way most people pay for utilities such as electricity and gas, that is, for usage only, not the entire plant.

The ASP value chain is an evolution of the traditional software model. Perhaps the most important competitive advantage of application services over traditional computing models is the lower cost of ownership. The savings derive from an ASP's ability to share the cost of expensive resources among a number of customers, rather than having to purchase and to maintain those resources separately. These savings are significantly enhanced if the ASP focuses on a specific range of application services. Since the most expensive resources for an IT provider are its skills and knowledge base, this effect is maximised by focusing on a specific application set and a precisely defined target group.

The ability to offer impeccable quality of service levels to customers depends not only on the providers of physical infrastructure but also on the way the infrastructure is managed. Indeed, some ASPs subcontract the hosting of their data centre to a specialist provider on the basis that their own core competence is applications management rather than data centre operations.

Where the ASP operates its own data centre, it must continue to invest in order to ensure that the facility keeps pace with the highest standards over time. Day-to-day management and control of the infrastructure must also use very sophisticated technology and be carried out according to strict quality management procedures.

Many of the success factors for an application service offering are established even before the first customer contract is signed. The selection of products and their preparation for the market is a critical ingredient. The ASP must select them to match its skill base and infrastructure and must then build an application service around them that matches the customer's requirements (see Figure 4.6.7).

The ASP's relationships with product vendors must be assured at least for the life of the contract to guarantee the availability of technical support services, product upgrades and ongoing staff training. With high-end application services an especially close relationship with vendors is likely to be necessary.

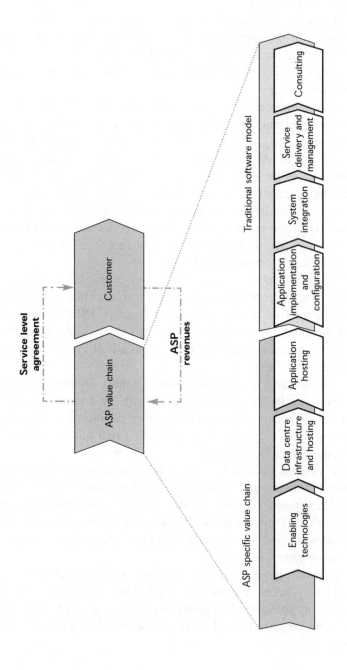

Figure 4.6.7 The ASP value chain

Service level agreement

Customer

ASP value chain

ASP revenues

Traditional software model

Consulting

Service delivery and management

System integration

Application implementation and configuration

Application hosting

Data centre infrastructure and hosting

Enabling technologies

ASP specific value chain

Positioning Siemens Business Services in today's ASP market

By understanding that the ASP has to make a significant commitment to an infrastructure and IT talent that is leverageable to serve multiple clients, SBS has already drawn activities to make the comprehensive know-how in professional services and in the integration business useful for the ASP business, that is:

- ASP consult – design – build – operate
- User-centred support
- Best-of-breed solutions
- Integration of business solutions
- Vertical segmentation.

The SBS ASP offering can be positioned in the market landscape as shown in Figure 4.6.8.

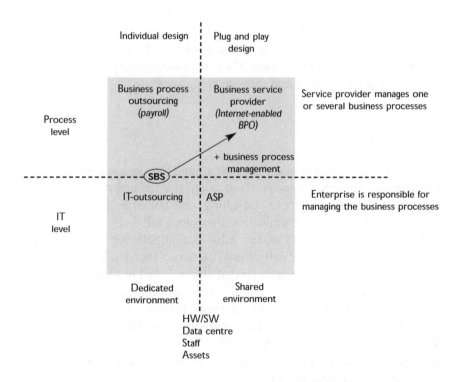

Figure 4.6.8   Positioning the SBS ASP offering

ASP consult – design – build – operate

SBS as a professional service company seeks to extend their service revenues into ASP offerings and to adapt partnership arrangements that complement the SBS expertise. Due to comprehensive experience in network services, data centre operation, application support, systems integration, and customer relationship, SBS is able to cover a wide range in the ASP value chain by delivering the full range of ASP back-up services or becoming a real front-end ASP (see Figure 4.6.9).

In 2000, UCS (User Centre Services) a business unit within SBS with heavy emphasis on outsourcing, business process outsourcing, out-tasking, and facilities management strongly focused on large enterprises, set up a project which is aimed at providing CRM business applications for midsize and small customers. Hereby, UCS has gained advantage by understanding the metrics of the business that basically drove the decision towards ASP services. Compared to the traditional UCS outsourcing business with customer-specific solutions, the new business is based on standardised applications for low cost and without any up-front investment for a large group of customers. UCS understood the advantages of network-based software usage. Beside fast implementation of new applications, customers can take advantage of reasonable and immediate access to brand new software innovations. Thus, expensive enterprise applications can also be used by small and midsize companies.

User-centred support

ASP customers expect help and support around the clock without having to use their own support resources which means that the major success criteria are qualified support, remote consulting, and online help as well as the provision of latest IP communication technology (IP multi-channel centre).

In these terms, the SBS added value is that SBS together with other partners is able to offer IP call centre functions. Thereby, the system integrates customer contacts across several channels and provides the contacts over the network. Additionally, the system distributes the contacts over customer support stations in the customer response centre. Due to long experience as an IT service provider and integrator, SBS was able to transform this know-how for the ASP customer response centre to have standardised services, process-oriented handling, and tool-supported procedures on a calculable cost basis.

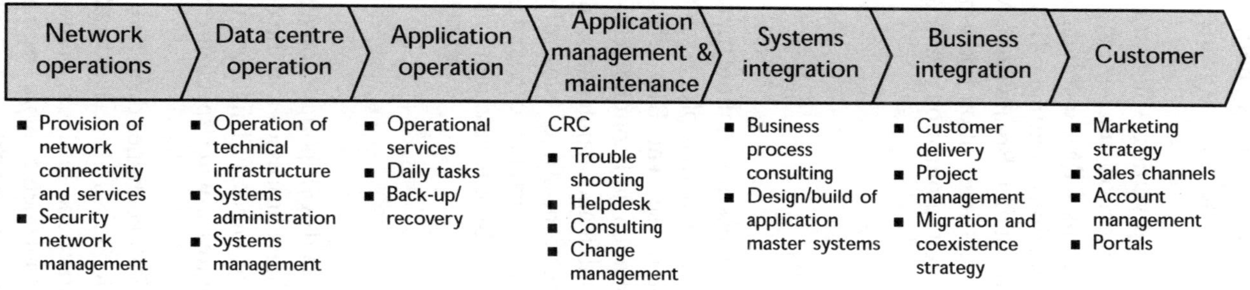

Network operations	Data centre operation	Application operation	Application management & maintenance	Systems integration	Business integration	Customer
■ Provision of network connectivity and services ■ Security network management	■ Operation of technical infrastructure ■ Systems administration ■ Systems management	■ Operational services ■ Daily tasks ■ Back-up/ recovery	CRC ■ Trouble shooting ■ Helpdesk ■ Consulting ■ Change management	■ Business process consulting ■ Design/build of application master systems	■ Customer delivery ■ Project management ■ Migration and coexistence strategy	■ Marketing strategy ■ Sales channels ■ Account management ■ Portals

Figure 4.6.9 The SBS ASP value chain

Best-of-breed solutions

ASP customers demand the best applications (horizontal or industry specific) for their business requirements with a justifiable price performance relation.

Over time, SBS has gathered deep vertical solution experience across many branches such as telecommunication, finance, and so on as well as horizontal solution experience such as CRM, e-commerce, collaborative applications, and personal applications. Further, SBS is a partner of leading software vendors like SAP, Siebel, Broadvision, Microsoft, and so on. This comprehensive solution and integration know-how is extremely useful for providing branch-tailored applications with a high degree of standardisation.

Integration of business solutions

SBS has developed the BIF (business integration framework) methodology which integrates internal and external processes and supports the seamless integration of the enterprise. The BIF offering includes the management of the whole information and communication infrastructure, outsourcing services for the operation and maintenance of data centres and remote network centres including front-office, back-office, helpdesk and first level support solutions as well as customer care and billing. This valuable methodology matches 1:1 the ASP business requirements.

Vertical segmentation

Vertically oriented marketplaces and ASP portals converge. The applications needed to optimise the business processes and the design of personal workplaces differ from industry to industry. This leads to the result that a wide ranging ASP offering requires a wide spectrum of horizontal and vertical applications.

The structure and skill set of SBS combines deep and versatile industry know-how with horizontal solution experience. This enables vertical ASP positioning through vertical market and business know-how. Hereby the vertical ASP approach can be supplemented with the essential horizontal solution requirements of the e-business world.

Conclusion

To be successful in the ASP business, a certified trained staff who can demonstrate experience in implementing and supporting the ASP's core applications is needed. Proven expertise in operating and managing a network-centric data centre in a server computing environment and demonstrable experience of managing service-based IT contracts are further key essentials. The configuration of a technical infrastructure that is clearly superior to that of a well equipped mid-market business and close relationships between the ASP and all its major suppliers are definitely required. The strategy and positioning of Siemens I&C regarding ASP business will certainly be influenced by the ability to become best in class provider either as a pure ASP or as a value-added service provider for other ASPs.

The e-roadmapping analysis

The Siemens case also presents a very distinct dimension to our strategy web. First, they are a bricks-and-mortar company truly leveraging their asset base to position themselves competitively in a very attractive future market. But more importantly, the project in question is at the time of the analysis still work in progress. Therefore we applied our e-roadmapping analysis only very selectively to the areas of customer centricity and technology as the most advanced areas.

eRI score

Applying our eRI Siemens achieved the scores shown in Figure 4.6.10 in the areas of customer centricity and technology.

We find Siemens scoring fairly highly in the sub-areas of customer intimacy, customer value, and brand.

- *Customer intimacy* – Given the history of the corporation and its diversified technology base, it is easy to understand how the Siemens ASP offering can start out with a very broad customer base and excellent customer access at its disposal. Needless to say, the current market research figures indicate the ASP market segment to be very prospective and lucrative.

- *Customer value* – With a complete product and service offering as described in the case, the company is well equipped and well positioned to offer the ASP customer all the products and service one requires. The nature of the business, furthermore, guarantees a fairly easily predictable flow of revenues, paired with continuous access to the customer. Considering, in addition, to what degree ASP

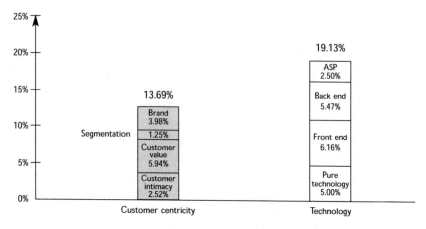

Figure 4.6.10   Siemens Business Services eRI score

offerings can even manage mission-critical applications, it is needless to say that through such an ASP offering, the Siemens company can get very close to the 'heart' of the ASP customer. Knowledge about usage patterns, customer behaviour up to a very refined level should be attainable, allowing subsequent service offerings to the customer.

- *Brand* – The third major pillar contributing to the fairly high customer centricity score is the Siemens brand. Although this offering is exclusively focused on B2B customers, bringing in this kind of brand opens doors. It opens doors where people are wary about ASP-ing mission-critical applications and Siemens can present their offering in conjunction with this very traditional, trusted brand image. And where customer relationships exist, past experiences of, for example, the technological savvy of Siemens, will enable fairly quick inroads to the customer in regard to the ASP offering.

The second pillar of importance in the ASP offering is the technology bid. As this ASP offering can be started with a green-field approach, and given the technological competence of Siemens, the ASP offering will satisfy all of the required major pureplay elements. These elements relate to scalability, compatibility, security, and portability. In all these technology areas, Siemens can offer state-of-the-art technology; either through inhouse competencies or through strategic partnerships as, for example, is done with Brokat AG for security concerns.

In conclusion, our eRI analysis detailed two major pillars of the company with a particular focus on customer centricity. The market for such an ASP offering is booming and the pre-conditions for a successful Siemens entry are present. Opportunities clearly lie in a professionalisation of the customer relationship and in the extension of the market segmentation. The ASP market will continue to gain importance, but it is unlikely that one player will be able to dominate the arena. More likely are scenarios of focused service providers, for example, in areas where technological expertise requires pairing with process and/or deep industry know-how.

The Quest for Total Connectivity

In the closing chapter of this book, we want to pick up on a theme that we used throughout the book and subsequently applied in our e-roadmapping process, and which we believe will become of greater importance in the future. The theme is connectivity. It is a theme that we believe all companies will need to consider in their e-roadmapping process, whether it will apply to the near- or long-term strategy horizon. Connectivity will be one of the most important forces in shaping the future digital landscape, and companies will need to understand the implications and possibilities of this dimension. Connectivity will by all means be the future basis for digital commerce.

Collaborative commerce

The basis for our belief and stressed importance of connectivity is the emerging trend and prediction of what some analysts have termed collaborative commerce, others are calling it collaborative hubs, e-hubs, e-markets, meta-mediaries, and so on. What is common to their divergent vocabulary is a belief that the future will bring more *integration* and *collaboration*.

The thought of integration pertains to the connection of currently separate processes, such as planning, forecasting, and transaction execution. And surely to really reap the benefits of electronic markets, most of the currently disconnected processes will need to be integrated. Why are the processes currently not integrated, one may ask? And the answer has to be twofold. First, most of the current online business transactions (B2B) are in areas of little strategic importance to companies. The typical first and second generation e-marketplace can offer unit and transaction cost savings within the area of MRO- (maintenance, repair and operations) and C-items (uncritical, non-production related goods). The procurement of these goods is usually executed on an ad hoc basis, might be governed by umbrella agreements but requires little to no integration with ERP (enterprise resource planning), MRP (material requirement planning) or SCM (supply chain management) systems. In addition, many 'critical' processes today are well organised along an outdated, closed and proprietary, yet functioning EDI system (electronic data interchange).

The second aspect to the lack of connectivity is the lack of agreement on technical standards for communicating between Internet-based transaction systems. This lack of technical standards, as one corporate put it, is surely 'non-trivial'. An overall agreement in the market can be found to the extent that all major players believe that the new standard will be based on XML (extensible markup language), a successor to the HTML programming language. The only problem is that many versions of XML exist and no one particular version seems to be able to secure domination, required for the establishment of a single standard. The key players in this arena are the non-profit organisations, like the W3C, who have no substantial stake in a particular operating software or procurement system, yet lack the full industry support for agreement and implementation of a single standard. The other kinds of player are typically industry consortia, like the IBM and Ariba-led UDDI initiative. Yet, all major players, like CommerceOne, had either previously launched a similar initiative or were in the process thereof. Some industry players even go so far as to suggest that current market conditions are not favourable to a single standard, implying that the current attempts of eight or more consortia to develop such a standard will be reduced to somewhere around possibly two standards.

The above-mentioned situation has led to two dilemmas. The first dilemma is an internal one: enabling existing ERP systems to communicate even basic information, like a uniform product description to a new web-based procurement engine, is another one of these non-trivial issues. And although the procurement system companies and middleware companies try to provide standard adapters allowing adequate conversion of their data, most companies which implemented ERP systems a few years beforehand took advantage of the possibilities of adapting these systems to their internal needs, disabling now most well-intended standard adapters towards the new procurement systems. This leaves most companies with the decision to add another free-standing application to their IT landscape, or go through the painful and expensive process of manually integrating both systems.

The second dilemma is of an external nature. Once a company has set up their system to work with one web-based procurement system, it cannot utilise marketplaces provided by competing procurement systems, nor can this company purchase materials from a supplier who is not utilising their particular procurement system. Some companies have tried to resolve this issue by attempting to attain critical mass of application of a single system in their vertical marketspace. However, the overall challenge of achieving connectivity across industries and product groups remains unsolved.

A graphical depiction of this current technology dilemma is provided in Figure 5.1. Take, for example, a financial services institution which has just implemented an Ariba procurement solution for the sourcing of their C-articles. First, internal processes were adapted and business procedures transferred to the rules engine of the software. In a next step, the relevant suppliers were told by which means and in what format their product offerings had to be integrated into the new catalogue system. After completion of this process the pre-specified groups of articles could now be ordered electronically from the pre-qualified and integrated suppliers. Let us now assume that this company wants to extend the product categories they source by these electronic means. And lo and behold, this bank finds a regional electronic marketplace already offering this extended product category via a range of integrated suppliers. Yet, this marketplace which offers the 'right' products runs on the 'wrong' platform, that is, a platform from a different software provider such as, for example, CommerceOne. Now many things can be done to remedy this situation but none of these is cheap or fast to implement.

Nevertheless, many software makers proclaim XML translation services will change this. What translation services will change, is that, for example, the bank could submit an Ariba purchase order for '20 red pencils', which the receiving party can open and read, yet no assurance is truly there that the *syntax* will be understood. Thus, in the best of cases the CommerceOne-based supplier will understand that an order of 20 pencils (irrespective of matching unique product codes) has been sent, but he could also receive a message that says a quantity of 20 writing instruments, which is not the level of certainty a purchase order should contain. If this level of certainty were to be transferred to the procurement of mission-critical goods, one can understand why seamless matchmaking is a few development stages away.

One can take this level of uncertainty one step further by illuminating the following two aspects. Keenan Vision (April and September 2000) suggested that of the currently 1000 worldwide marketplaces, we will see an increase to over 4000 by the year 2004. Couple this notion with the following fact and one can see the great potential of our collaborative commerce vision, but also the great many efforts still required. Berlecon Research (July 2000) found that of the roughly 130 German-speaking marketplaces, over 75 per cent are not run on standard software, but on self-developed software engines or parts of standard components.

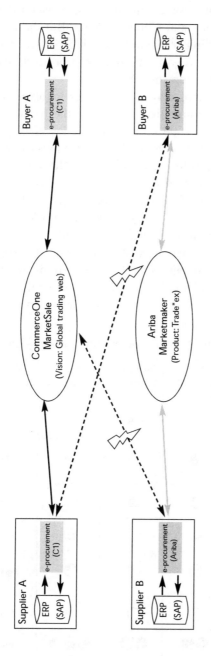

Figure 5.1 Current market landscape

Therefore, collaborative commerce is not just a matter of designing a standard translation adapter for communication between the two major marketplace providers Ariba and CommerceOne. But the task at hand is potentially one of providing translation services between hundreds of different software engines, all with different software code specifications, on top of using different versions of XML.

To depict the complexity of players and issues involved in the discussion around XML-based transaction standards, the reader may refer to Table 5.1. The chart lists a wide array of examples of players having a substantial stake in this debate. These classes of players range from non-profit standard-setting bodies like XML.org, over ERP systems, web-based procurement systems to infrastructure players like British Telecom or Deutsche Telekom. In view of the players involved and the stake at hand (particularly the future stake) one can now surely understand why an agreement on standards is far away, if feasible at all.

The vision of integration becomes of even greater importance for the wave of digital business, if one considers the current market situation. Most of the press has for a long time been proclaiming the upside of B2C ventures, like Amazon but most profit potential has been attributed to the

Table 5.1   Competition for domination through standards

Criterion / Competitors	RosettaNet XML.org	SAP PeopleSoft JDE	OnDisplay Vignette Nimble	Ariba Commerce One	BEA Neon	BT Dt. Telekom
Standard-bridging	◕	O	◔	◔	O	O
Business processes and content	◑	◕	O	◑	◔	O
Intelligent agent (pull)	O	◔	◕	O	O	◔
Web front-end	O	◕	O	●	O	O
Middleware/ systems integration	O	◔	◔	◔	◕	◔
Infrastructure provision	O	O	O	◔	O	●
Score	●◔	●●	●◔	●●◔	●	●◑

Key   O = 1   ◔ = 2   ◑ = 3   ◕ = 4   ● = 5

Level of competency   O = none   ◔ = low   ◑ = modest   ◕ = high   ● = full

B2B ventures, as the figures clearly indicate in Figure 5.2. Nevertheless, even the highly promising B2B marketplaces have not been able to generate the traffic and critical mass that many entrepreneurs had planned for and many analysts had predicted. The reasons for this delta of projection and reality are surely manifold, but often rest with the lack of particular functional or industry experience on the side of the marketplace providers. And on the user side we find many corporations which are fairly late into the electronic business arena and are now overwhelmed with the quantity of marketplace offerings on the one hand and the launch of their very own e-business on the other hand.

The aforementioned lack of liquidity and traffic on these markets is an overarching phenomenon, with notable exceptions. Reliable figures on this delta of projection vs. reality are currently not readily available, which from an investor and company perspective is understandable. Yet, from our interviews with many European B2B marketplace providers, the majority of companies will in private confide that the potential is there, but that sales are not materialising at the rate they were projected.

The second aspect of collaborative commerce is *collaboration*. For effective collaboration to take place the aforementioned integration and provision of connectivity is a pre-condition. Collaboration means even more efficient and effective processes. Collaborative commerce is the evolutionary step up from procurement of MRO articles to allocation of mission critical goods (A- and B-articles) and integration of central business processes. The suggestion of efficiency and effectiveness gains needs to be further elaborated on.

The *efficiency* gain is somewhat along the reasoning of these first generation marketplaces, that is, procuring A- or B-articles over meta-markets

Global volume in $ billions

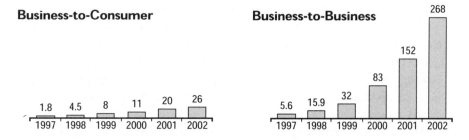

Figure 5.2   B2C and B2B statistics

Source: Forrester Research

will require some further degrees of standardisation. This standardisation should help to reduce unit cost and will therefore help to increase efficiencies. Additional efficiency gains are to be expected through the technologically based integration of the various back-end, front-end and web systems. Savings should incur from the availability of single data sources, and so on.

The *effectiveness* gain, however, is the more promising. Seamless integration of back-end systems up to marketplace systems allows for the better design of interaction. This clearly implies the redesign possibilities for most value chains. Whereas, for example, today a car manufacturer will issue a materials request to a systems supplier only when the acute need arises, this often means shifting the cost of material availability to the systems supplier and/or suppliers further down the food chain. This leads mostly to one-way communications and the necessity of suppliers maintaining some sort of sensible market forecasting system, which signifies a high degree of inefficiency.

Integrated systems should allow all suppliers of the manufacturer to partake in the manufacturer's planning process, that is, the supplier finds out about the big picture needs exactly at the same time as the manufacturer takes that decision. This will enable overall more effective processes with possibilities of feedback- and learning-loops, and it will allow removal of further inefficiencies in the production process. This integration of processes applies not only to mere production but also to all other related processes, such as R&D, sales and marketing, and logistics.

One can easily comprehend that the basis for such a vision is the aforementioned common technological basis. However, experts concur that only 20 per cent of this vision are a question of technology, the other 80 per cent are business processes. Hence, the need to tackle these 80 per cent as soon as possible.

These 80 per cent business processes consist of two major components: the process and its steps, and the contents and its parameterisation.

The *process* and its steps will need to be newly defined in a collaborative commerce setting. The definition of these processes and the subsequent process steps will most likely have to be confined to the realms of industry or community segments. This is particularly true if this argument is to be applied to mission-critical processes and the procurement of A- and B-articles.

The advent of technologically enabled collaborative commerce will ease the phasing out of traditional processes, as all players have much to gain from these newly designed processes and very few of the old processes will be of value. A simple concretisation of the benefits of the new process and the little good of old processes was elaborated on before, detailing common forecasting. In addition, if the basis of technological integration and connectivity is made available, most industry players will have no choice but to join the new process design efforts, as the competitive pressure and particularly the expected benefits from collaborative commerce will enable companies to realise substantial and measurable results.

The *content* part of the 80 per cent business processes is the second critical issue. Once the steps and sequence of a process have been decided, one must then determine what content each process step has to include. In other words, once the step of issuing a purchase order (PO) is in place, the question now becomes, how can this PO be parameterised so that all involved parties can not only understand the content, but also make productive use of it. And again, deciding the specifics of this content will most likely be first of all governed by the various industry/community segments.

The challenge at hand is to define these new processes and the content parameterisation at a sensible time-to-market speed, that is, the three-year cycles of general approval we all remember from the EDI days of agreeing on a purchase order format are no longer acceptable.

Below we summarise the three components the collaborative commerce vision needs to entail (cf. Figure 5.3).

The first step is connectivity: today, only users of the same software configurations can use electronic procurement and marketplace solutions. That is to say, only users of the Ariba procurement system can order from an Ariba marketplace, they cannot however order from a CommerceOne-based marketplace. This eliminates true supplier choice and creates substantial switching cost. Tomorrow's connectivity technology will create a common basis for connection and subsequently solve this problem.

The second step is processes: today the linking of, for example, purchasing processes is mostly done on the basis of buyer-specified process steps. Supplying the same goods – even by the same means – to a different buyer typically will require the supplier to adhere to a different process. Creating industry-specific common process types will resolve this problem. Most processes of transaction today can be differentiated according to the importance of these goods (A-, B-, and C-goods) and the respective transaction execution. Coupling this prioritisation with an industry-specific transaction execution mechanism in the form of industry-wide agreed-upon processes would be the favourable solution.

The third step solves the content issue: most purchase orders today carry the format that the company once specified during the implementation of their ERP system, resulting in an unmanageable amount of diverging purchase orders. Industry-wide agreement on the necessary

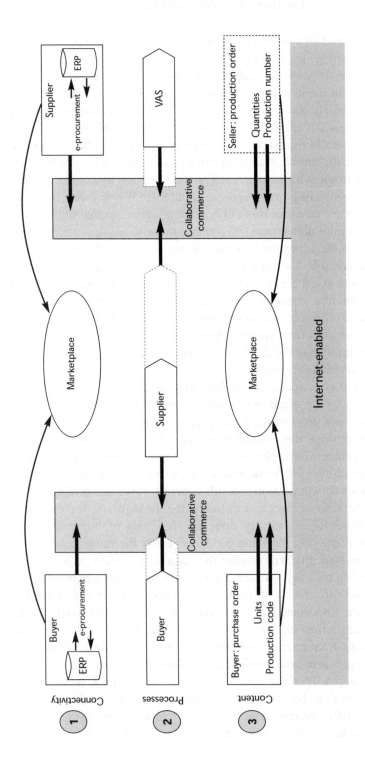

Figure 5.3 Components of the collaborative commerce vision

content requirements and the specific parameterisation will render this topic solved and create a more efficient standardised process flow.

So why would anyone even consider participating in these efforts entailing a complete redesign of processes, process content, and a new technological infrastructure?

First, the direct benefits are fairly straightforward and measurable, and most competitive environments will entice single industry players to reap the benefits of such a new tool. These benefits will stem from the newly designed more efficient and effective processes and the implied seamlessness of processes; something that was promised early on in the Internet, but never materialised in a satisfactory manner. One may consider the sum of these factors also as a push factor.

The other major benefit, our pull factor, is the switching costs. With existing EDI solutions in place for the procurement of mission-critical goods, no complete calculation can be presented that would entice companies to switch to an Internet-based system. The new technology and tool will create this enticement from a profit perspective, yet even more important is the fact that switching costs in a collaborative commerce setting are close to zero. Once a common technological basis is in place, processes and content agreed upon, the whole universe is at your disposal and can be communicated with. It will make no difference how long, for example, a supplier relationship has existed, or whether you are using SAP and your potential new partner Oracle. The three elements of collaborative commerce will enable you to communicate across histories and systems.

This factor of lacking switching cost within collaborative commerce will give companies the assurance of having committed to the right 'game' and no further scare of technological lock-in or ceasing application providers will exist.

This fear of technological lock-in or even betting on the wrong horse altogether (remember Baan?!) now no longer exists. Current decisions to, for example, add a customer relationship management (CRM) system have in the past often been made, based on a previous decision for a particular ERP system and the availability of CRM tools from the ERP provider. Again, a previous decision will no longer prohibit a future decision for the best product, as the major issue, true connectivity, can finally be solved.

Once all three levels of connectivity (technological, process, and content standard) are achieved the following vision of collaborative commerce in action will become reality (Figure 5.4).

This vision of reality focuses on the ultimate connection of the buyer with the supplier. Everything else needed to fulfil and execute this transaction will be provided for on the collaborative commerce platform, as no

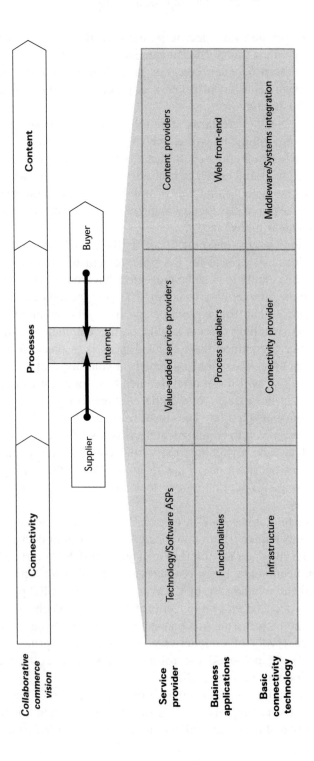

Figure 5.4 Vision of collaborative commerce in action

particular steps on the side of the participants will have to be taken. As Bear Sterns noted in a recent report (Summer 2000) 'B2B is fundamentally about Web-based software tied together and delivered through public and private marketplaces'. As this is very much in line with our vision, Bear Sterns continues to assert '(v)ery little of the infrastructure and applications needed to automate business processes and relationships outside the enterprise are in place today'. While we concur with this opinion, we believe one way forward is to concretise the vision of collaborative commerce.

To beef up our vision of collaborative commerce, we deem the following architecture and dimensions of interaction sensible. The *basic connectivity technology* level has three parts: the first one is physical infrastructure and contains all of the necessary wiring and hardware; the second provides for inter-organisational connectivity consisting of some hardware but mostly software; and the third level assures intra-organisational integration of heterogeneous systems through software adapters.

The *business application* part could consist of a front-end functionality including a graphical interface, integration of corporate design, and so on. The second part would facilitate all necessary business functionalities, including materials planning, accounting and financials, and so on, while the third part would enable a process flow of this business application part.

The *service provider* dimension would include all parties providing the basics, for example, business software on an ASP basis. The second dimension would include all providers of value-added services, ranging from information-based services, such as credit checking, to asset-flow-based services, such as overseas logistics services. The last dimension integrates all of the more operational outsourced content providers, differentiating the content dimension from the previous value-added services dimension.

As we can see in Figure 5.5, one can easily validate this map of complementarities detailing the required players for realising the collaborative commerce vision from today's landscape of competitors.

For example, infrastructure is and will remain a core topic for the likes of British Telecom and Cisco, while EAI (enterprise application integration) providers like BEA are very much at home in the systems integration area. Likewise, SAP is one of today's key providers of business functionalities, while firms like i2 help enable effective and efficient supply chain processes. In the service provision arena, players like marchFIRST are establishing their very own ASP service offerings, while firms like Deutsche Post are already riding high in their role of value-added service provision.

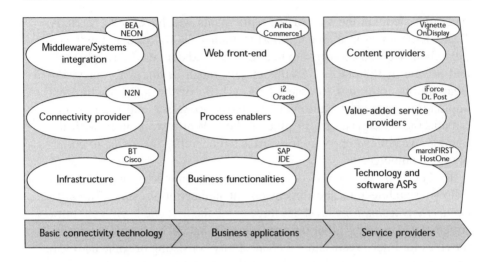

Figure 5.5   Strategic complementarity map for
collaborative commerce vision

What is now needed is agreement on the value of the vision of collaborative commerce and the joint steps some of these competing players will have to take.

Our understanding of collaborative commerce outlined how this vision could become reality through the three steps of connectivity and integration, process and value chain redesign, and content parameterisation and standardisation. Concretising that in an architecture and mapping today's players to the requirements make this vision appear attainable in the near future.

Summary

The closing comments of this chapter will sum up the essential arguments for our prediction that connectivity will become the next major thing that corporations of all sizes and flavour need to integrate into their strategising efforts. Failure to do so will reduce a firm's ability to compete on a level playing field within a short period of time. The possibilities of connectivity are great enough for many companies to participate, yet the urge to be one of the shaping forces, particularly behind the process and content bid is absolutely necessary.

In this chapter we showed that the Internet helps create true transparency, real-time matchmaking and industrial strength liquidity, in the end facilitating better demand and supply. However, these improvements of general e-procurement only proved valid for MRO parts. Moreover, problems of fulfilment integration and systems incompatibility held savings low. Integration efforts will help unlock the true potential of e-procurement by providing a technology-based common XML standard (uniting the current eight and more competing standards), in addition to facilitating industry-specific unique processes and standardised content containers, for example, for a generic PO.

In the end result, this will enable, for example, all Ariba front-end users to source across the universe of all Internet-connected suppliers, and not as currently, only across the universe of Ariba-connected suppliers.

Then, with the emergence of collaborative commerce in the coming years, seamless connectivity will be the pre-condition, entailing an XML-based technological standard, unique processes, and standardised content.

The future holds great potential for true interactivity, that is, intelligent agents find your demand-specific supply; this requires much greater demands for connectivity and seamless operational fulfilment. Today's marketplaces offer C-part and spot transactions; collaborative commerce will enable A- and B-part transaction as seamless integration with back-end systems can be achieved. Today, the underlying technological switching costs are too high and thus corporations will not commit business-critical processes; collaborative commerce through its strategic positioning will reduce these costs to near zero. The coming standard is XML, yet at least eight major versions of XML exist; none of these players (like Microsoft or Ariba) can in these times of monopoly aversion credibly attempt the creation of a global standard, and more importantly, the issue of XML standards is only 20 per cent technology related but 80 per cent process related.

The collaborative commerce value proposition is true connectivity for all functional (sourcing, matchmaking up to fulfilment) business processes, across industries.

The benefits of the collaborative commerce model are real market efficiencies (that is, a true supplier universe available on real-time demand), cost savings (that is, cheap transactions and goods), new sales channels (being connected facilitates constant 'offerings'), and elimination of technological lock-in through the near-zero reduction of switching cost.